A life with

*un*certainty

MY STORY OF LIVING
WITH SCLERODERMA

A Life With Uncertainty
Copyright © 2021 by Claudia Sultan.

This is a work of nonfiction. The events and conversations in this book have been set down to the best of the author's ability, although some names and details may have been changed to protect the privacy of individuals. Every effort has been made to trace or contact all copyright holders. The publishers will be pleased to make good any omissions or rectify any mistakes brought to their attention at the earliest opportunity.

Printed in Australia

First Printing: July 2021

SHAWLINE
PUBLISHING
GROUP

Shawline Publishing Group Pty Ltd
www.shawlinepublishing.com.au

Paperback ISBN- 9781922444790
Ebook ISBN- 9781922444806

ACKNOWLEDGMENTS;

To my family,

I have been blessed with the greatest gift, a loving and supportive family. Thank you for helping me fight my battles and provide comfort along the way.

Thank you for being my everything. My heart is filled with so much love and joy.

You are my rock, my strength and smile, you are forever in my heart.

To Dr John Moore & Dr Helen Englert,

Thank you for your hard work and ongoing support. I am filled with immense gratitude for your efforts in keeping me alive. Thank you with all my heart. You are a part of an amazing team and doctors like you make the world a better place.

To the Stem Cell Transplant team at St Vincent's Hospital—thank for your support, kindness and efforts during my stay at the hospital.

To Dr Christopher Browne,

Thank you for encouraging me to participate in the stem cell transplant and helping me to find the light at the end of the tunnel.

To Dr Longin Zurek,

Words cannot express how grateful I am for your kindness, thoughtfulness, and ongoing generosity. Thank you for being you.

To my dear friends Neal Vanzleve & Andrew Howison,

Thank you for your support, kindness and encouragement. Your friendship means so much to me.

CONTENTS

A life with uncertainty

MY STORY OF LIVING WITH SCLERODERMA

CLAUDIA SULTAN

PART 1: OLD CLAUDIA

I AM AUSTRALIAN born with a Lebanese Muslim heritage. I am one of five. Growing up with three brothers and one sister was a great experience. My siblings and I are very close and we spent plenty of time together growing up in our solid and stable environment.

Like all siblings, we fought over the remote control and constantly played pranks on each other. At times my parents would sometimes call us by the wrong names. We loved one another but didn't stop us getting in each other's way, dobbing on each other or harassing one another, making faces or nasty comments while our parents were still in the room. There were times I would have to share my toys with my sister and she would refuse to give them back, and I would throw a fit and she would start crying. As we grew older I would catch my sister trying to squeeze into my clothing, being unreasonable and hoping the dress would fit her. These were all good, fun times but we always made sure we had each other's back. I know at some point we drove my mother mad, and no doubt she probably wanted to pull her hair out. Nevertheless, it was a home filled with joy, laughter and plenty of love. I guess you could say I had a very entertaining childhood. The kind any kid would ask for.

I was a stubborn and selfish child. If I wanted something, I had to have it. On one occasion, my mother took my older brother and I to the shopping centre, she was pregnant with our sister and we caught the bus to the mall with as little as $48.00 in our wallet. I was walking between the clothes racks, and my big brown eyes landed on a black one-piece bathing-suit with colourful bright stars all over it. I had to have it. Mum couldn't afford to buy it, but that didn't stop me from throwing a tantrum. I stamped my feet and started crying. I had an emotional meltdown; I didn't particularly have them often… frustrated and embarrassed by my emotional rage in store, mum pulled out her wallet to purchase the bathing suit. With very little money left in mum's wallet, we walked home on foot that day as mum struggled to push the baby stroller up the hill. When my mother shared this story with me, I felt a sense of guilt, shame and embarrassment for my behaviour as a child and my first thought was to apologise to mum and express remorse, but instead we had a few laughs and hugged it out.

I've always had this obsession with swimming pools. We couldn't afford to build one or buy a home with a pool, but my old primary school had a pool and I often attended the weekly swimming lessons. I wasn't particularly thrilled about learning how to swim; I was always afraid to get into the water. My teacher was a bit rough, she sensed my fear and anxiety, and pressed on it by dragging me into the shallow end of the pool and trying to teach me to paddle but I refused to let go of her arm. When she tried to get me to float on my back, I still wouldn't let go. With the teacher's support, I paddled to the edge of the pool and clung to the wall as my feet dangled in the water and held tightly as I made my way to the pool ladder. This one time, I was sitting on the edge of the swimming pool with my legs crossed at the knee, I leaned forward to run my hands through the water when I accidentally fell into the pool. I was unable to scream or shout for help. I panicked; my chest felt so tight. I didn't know how to swim, and had been too fearful to learn up until that moment. I was so frightened that I swallowed a small amount of water before I resurfaced and found the pool ladder. I gripped it to pull myself out of the pool and coughed up chlorinated water. I looked around to see if the other children had noticed that I had fallen in the pool, it seemed that nobody had noticed including the teacher.

I am fortunate to be blessed with the most amazing parents. The two most influential people in my life taught us the important values and lessons of life. Growing up, we always had plenty, but with only one income coming through mum always made sure we had the best of everything, most importantly shelter, food, clothes and good education. An education that my parents missed out on that would have definitely made life a lot easier for them, but circumstances made it impossible for both of my parents to achieve their lifelong goals.

Thanks to mum and dad, we learnt to appreciate the hard work that comes with raising a family, the sacrifices they've made to provide for us and their strong efforts to raise such honest, caring and loyal children. These two beautiful souls are perfect role models, their endless love, affection, compassion and ongoing support is never ending. As grown adults, my parents continue to inspire us to be the better versions of ourselves, with a little nudge of encouragement and support that never goes astray.

After completing high school, I went to University to study Psychology. Four years later graduated with my bachelors' degree and found a job in Sydney. Life was good, and I was moving up in the corporate space. My focus and priority was my career.

I lived a socially active life, and I enjoyed it. I was fit, but I rarely exercised. I was a strong healthy soul with a nice physique and naturally good looks. I enjoyed watching movies, reading, swimming, playing baseball and bike riding. As much as I enjoyed outdoor activities, camping is certainly is not one of them, it's never been my thing and I would hate to sleep on the ground. It's so uncomfortable, how could I live without a bathroom? Please, don't get me started on the mosquitoes and wild animals out there. I am happy to be dropped off at a local motel and regroup the next day.

I've always enjoyed dancing, it's one thing my sister and I share in common, casual dancing and busting a move here and there, listening to my playlist songs from the 80s and 90s. It wasn't much of a competition, but it was fun and we bonded. Our fascination of dancing opened our hearts to modern classic ballroom dancing. I purchased the DVD *Strictly Ballroom*, fell in love with Paul Mercurio's (who plays Scott Hastings) good looks and dreamt I was his Fran. I never got sick of watching this movie, and we'd wait for the credits roll in as we listened to the soulful voice of John Paul Young singing *Loves in the Air* and waltz around the living room and kitchen singing and laughing until the song ended.

I was very fond of skating. It was one of the most invaluable parts of my life. I still remember my first skates. I won them at a Christmas event. They were white with pink laces and black wheels. I learnt to skate on the road and the footpath, which frustrated my mother. All too often, I'd fall over and walk home in my white socks, carrying my skates in my hands. The first time I fell over, mum threw out my skates and so I persuaded dad to buy me a new pair of skates and promised to only skate in the driveway, which obviously caused my parents to clash. Undoubtedly, my father and I share a special bond; our bond is so strong, sacred and beautiful. I love the uniqueness of our relationship. We have a lot in common, dad always made time for my siblings and I. He is a loving and supportive father and always makes us feel our thoughts and opinions matter. Dad had all kind of stories to share about his childhood experiences, good and bad, we would listen carefully and wait until he'd finished before we asked our questions.

I'd always considered myself dad's little girl and as I grew older our close relationship naturally continued. Whatever problem I had, I would confide in Dad, he held all my secrets. Then there were days when mum and I would fight, and dad was always caught between us. But he always made sure we sorted out our differences.

My mother has always been my devoted supporter and the most important woman in my life. We also share a powerful bond which is built upon unconditional love and respect.

I have always idolized my mother.. My mother has always provided us a foundation of love, communication and guidance, offering advice when needed. We may be of two different generations, but notably we are best friends. There is a lot about her that makes her uniquely awesome, and I adore her to bits. My mother is naturally beautiful, she will walk into a room and her smile is enough to brighten up the place. She never sees the bad in people and tends to make excuses for their actions and behaviours. Some people take advantage of her kindness, but she is always forgiving. Our time together is always precious, I've learnt early on to make each moment count.

Growing up with three brothers helped me to become the strong independent woman I am today. I found myself engaged in all sort of activities; I would accept a challenge of football, ride a bicycle over a plank with bricks, steal passionfruit from a neighbour's tree, build a cubby house from tree branches and bricks laying around anything we could possibly find, door knocking, arm wrestling, playing soccer in the front yard, climbing a tree, filling up water balloons and tagging each other, playing with nerf guns, and Mortal Kombat and Mario on the Nintendo. It was fun but always competitive, and there was no such thing as rules. However, if I didn't accept any of these challenges I would become the target of their series of pranks and blackmail schemes. As we got older, we had no time for such games and became busy with grown-up things.

I was an adventurous soul. I used every opportunity to get out and have some fun. One of the most thrilling and craziest things I have ever done was in my early twenties, I went skydiving with a group of friends and it was the greatest experience ever. I was nervous leading up to it, but once we got on the plane I was ready to give it a shot. I was the first to jump out with a group of young girls cheering me on in the background, 'Go Claudia'. When the rear exit door opened, a rush of cold wind hit me in the face and instantly I grabbed hold of the instructor's arm and blurted out, 'I don't think I can do this.' Meanwhile, I could hear my friends shouting out words of encouragement. I was so scared but excited, so I decide to continue on with the mission. The instructor nudged me towards to the open door. My arms were crossed, my knees were bent, my eyes were closed and we jumped out.

Just like that, it happened so quickly.

Skydiving is inherently scary and I screamed. The falling

sensation was unbelievable, words cannot explain it. It was so windy and cold and I felt my face being stretched. Repeatedly the instructor told me to raise my head and look at the camera, but I couldn't even control my face, the only expression I wore was fear.

Growing up into a large-extended loving Lebanese-Australian family has its pros and cons. There are many role models, generations gaps, and a lot of inside family stories that are funny and tend to change over the years. Be prepared for unannounced house visits at any time of the day or night. Some of us live in the same neighbourhood, same suburb or twenty minutes' drive away. For starters, there are so many of us to mingle with *(don't get me started on the number of cousins I have, my first friends were my cousins)*, and if you get sick of one person, you can always move on to the next. I know it's a bit harsh, but it's reality. There is a large emotional support network available to you, they are willing to help, listen and offer you the best advice ever. You are never alone. There are plenty of celebrations including gatherings such as barbeques, birthdays, weddings and graduations and we always look forward to eating together. Your family are your biggest fans and cheerleaders.

But on the downside, everyone knows your business. By the end of day or week, (depending on how quickly news travels) everyone will know your secrets because family gossip never ends. There's nothing quite like when members of the family look at you with blank faces and raise their eyebrows, and respond with comments like, 'OMG we didn't know' when *of course* they already knew.

It's almost unavoidable to have a gathering with no family gossip. Honestly, I don't mind. It makes these gatherings quite entertaining. Almost six hours later conversations often end with, 'let's not talk, God will judge us.' As the saying goes, no family is perfect, right? I love them to bits and I wouldn't have it any other way.

We are a LOUD bunch. The volume of our voices is so high, that sometimes I am unable to hear myself think. Chatter diverges into big conversations where we passionately argue or debate about something, and you often need to raise your voice to be heard.

Or someone like an aunty, uncle or grandma suggesting ways to further improve yourself... Heaven forbid you invite one half of the family to a gathering and fail to invite the rest. All will be offended, and no doubt it will be the topic of conversation for the rest of the week. It always takes at least ten to fifteen minutes to say goodbye... why so long?

If you marry a Lebanese man or woman, you'll be married to his or her extended family too!

My intense fear of cats began when I was fourteen years old. There lived an old lady in my street who owned many cats. One afternoon my mum handed me an Avon catalogue and instructed me to place the it on the lady's doormat, but instead I knocked on her door and waited until she opened it. When she opened the door and I looked inside to see cats everywhere. She had cats on the sofa, the floor, kitchen bench, one sitting on top of the bulky tv, cats standing near the doorway with a giant litter box in the middle of the living room. The house reeked of cats. I dropped the catalogue on the mat and ran home. That night I dreamt I was walking home from the bus stop and her cats attacked me. The following day my old brother and I got off the school bus and making our way home, when we saw the old lady standing on her porch with a cane in her hand, and a dog laying at her feet. I was surprised to see her outside of the house, but she mumbled something to the dog and the little beast somehow crossed the road and chased after my older brother and I. We both ran home screaming for help. When I looked back to see how close the dog was, the old lady stood there on the footpath laughing at our misery. It wasn't until I reached the white fence of our home I felt a massive weight on my back and fell to the ground. When I looked up, our neighbour's black dog was hovering over my head. I screamed until I could no longer hear my own voice. By this point mum had come to my aid and I was trembling in fear. Even today, I am still afraid of cats and they cause me anxiety.

The Lebanese culture is made up of rich Lebanese cuisine. I grew up in a family with a deep passion for cooking and recipes that have been passed down from generation to generation. Our kitchen comes to life when mum is cooking one of her famous dishes. Mum cooks with love, which is why the food tastes so good. She has always been an amazing cook, something that comes to her so naturally. Despite her mood, she always finds comfort in the kitchen. She is always serving up a new dish and always has fun with her new creations. No dish is simple with mum. I am still learning the basics, something I haven't quite grasped yet from my talented mother, as I am still trying to find my way around the kitchen.

As long as I can remember, mum has been preparing my lunch for work. Before I leave the house, I have two containers of traditional Lebanese food with me and that's just for lunch. Fortunately, gaining weight has never been an underlying issue for me. I can pretty much eat whatever I want, I had a fast metabolism, so never had to worry about food. I was never embarrassed about eating four slices of pizza on a date. If I was hungry, I would eat.

We all joke about having a sweet tooth, but I do. Eating sweets and chocolate has always been my weakness; I struggle to resist anything sweet. As I recall, I was the little girl who sat under my grandparent's kitchen table licking and sucking on sugar cubes. As an adult, I find it almost impossible to avoid sugar. I have jars of lollies on my desk at work and a block of chocolate in my drawer for backup.

Though these events may seem somewhat disconnected, they're all a part of what my life was like before I got sick.

It was the winter of 2013, cold chilly morning. I'd been up since 5am getting ready for work. I just made myself a cup of tea and some toast. I sat in front of the heater enjoying the warm air on my face. I looked outside the window and the clouds outside were black and the rain made tracks down the pane of glass. I was annoyed that I had spent a good forty minutes straightening my hair and now the slightest drop of rain would frizz it up. Growing up with thick curly hair was exhausting and required a lot of maintenance, sometimes it felt like it was a curse. Mum would iron out my hair, but it wasn't long before we discovered the hair straightener and mum bought one immediately.

I had to find an umbrella before I could leave the house. There were seven people living at home and we didn't have one umbrella that wasn't half broken. I grabbed one of the few umbrellas we had and made my way to the car with my older brother. It was a challenge to get in the car without getting my hair wet, with one side of the umbrella plumped high and the other side collapsed. It was a cheap umbrella that had to be thrown out. Luckily, I always carry a can of hairspray with me. I decided that once I got into the office, I would spray down my hair and pin it back.

Today I was travelling to work with my older brother, we just got on the train and I pulled out a romance novel, *Captive Bride* by Rosemary Carter. He just shook his head and leaned over to whisper, 'Seriously what is wrong with you, who reads at this hour?' But I was determined to continue reading, I had to know if Liane accepted Kyle's proposal.

Some of the commuters were snoring, others were sleeping with their mouths wide open and the rest just sat there quietly playing with their phones, reading a book or watching a movie on their laptops or iPads. Don't get me wrong, I love sleep, but I slept a good eight hours and I was eager to read the next chapter of my book before I got into the office. Before I opened my book, I glanced over at my brother and saw that his were arms folded across his chest, head down and eyes shut.

Monday morning, I stood outside my office building lighting up my Winston super slim cigarette. I had just purchased an English breakfast tea with four sugars and milk. It was raining heavily with strong winds. I looked at the weather forecast and we were facing much more miserable weather for the rest of the week. The traffic moved slowly, people were moving between the traffic to get into their offices. It was chaos; the trains were delayed this morning, signals were down, and by the time I got into the office it was almost 9:30am. I was wearing a soft cream, thick winter coat I had purchased the weekend before. It was worth every penny spent. Back in the office, my matching cream gloves lay on my desk.

After my cigarette, I noticed something quite odd about my fingers. The colour of my fingertips had changed to blue. I was surprised, but I overlooked it.... A few days passed and the same thing happened again, only this time I was in the office sitting behind my desk. The feeling in my fingers became all numb, and my fingers suddenly changed colour again. It was at that moment I realised something was not right with my body. Although I didn't know it then, it was my first signs of Raynaud's disease.

I consulted with my local GP, who referred me on to a vascular specialist. The specialist examined my fingers and confirmed that I have Raynaud's syndrome and referred me to a rheumatologist who could help treat my condition. When I first got diagnosed with Raynaud's disease, I knew very little about the disease. After some research, I came to understand Raynaud's and the common symptoms. Raynaud's is a process in which the fingers and or toes change colour in response to cold temperatures or emotional distress. It is also associated with throbbing pain of pins and needles sensation. During a Raynaud's attack, there is limited blood circulation to the fingers and or toes. At the end of attack, the fingers turn red again, which means the blood is flowing back through to the fingers.

As weeks progressed, my fingers continued to discolour. I tried all types of treatments to help keep my fingers warm and stop the throbbing pain, but nothing seemed to work. I found it difficult to perform daily tasks when Raynaud's attacked. I used hand warmers to keep my fingers warm, but the discomfort was unpleasant, especially when circulation returned. I immediately ceased smoking. The rheumatologist prescribed calcium channel blockers to help increase blood flow to the fingers and ease the Raynaud's attack. One of the side effects was hot flushes. I was terribly afraid to lose a finger.

One morning I woke up with severe joint pain in my wrists and ankles. There was some swelling. My rheumatologist prescribed 25mg of prednisone to help reduce and ease the inflammation, but instead I gained some weight and experienced rapid mood swings.

Things progressed quickly, and by late November 2013 I was officially diagnosed with Systemic Scleroderma, a chronic autoimmune disease referring to hard skin, known for tightening of the skin associated with joint pain and fatigue.

I had received the worst news ever. I was in shock. What was I supposed to do now? I was trying to make sense of what the rheumatologist was saying. My head was spinning. Mum and I sat there in silence. We were both lost for words. There was no cure, and life expectancy after the onset of the disease is anything between five to fifteen years. Just listening to rheumatologist convey the words, 'autoimmune disease', 'body attacks itself', 'skin thickens,' 'organ failure,' 'death,' made me sick in the stomach. I was too young to die; I could not understand why this was happening to me. I was overwhelmed with emotions, too worried and scared of what was yet to come. I looked over to where my mother was sitting and her eyes were filled with tears.

I was devastated to learn I had scleroderma, a fatal disease that could only be managed with medications, and life expectancy was short. The truth is, I didn't really grasp the severity of the disease until I started reading up on scleroderma, and learning about the symptoms and horrors of the disease. There was so much uncertainty with the disease, my future was now unknown.

My life priorities had suddenly changed and there was little I could do, but wait for it to unravel. The struggle for survival suddenly became too real.

Scleroderma is a rare autoimmune disease in which the immune system attacks its own body without warning. A chronic illness that produces too much collagen in the body, that results in thickness of skin causing damage to the connective tissue. This could lead to internal damage of the organs such as lungs, heart, kidneys, gastrointestinal and oesophagus.

The severity of scleroderma varies between people, depending how much of the skin is really affected. For some it can be manageable, and for others it can be life threatening. I knew nothing about the disease. I had never heard of the word scleroderma. After relentless hours of researching, I came to understand there is no cause or cure for the disease. Not knowing the cause and learning there is no cure drove me to despair.

Scleroderma occurs in people between the ages of thirty to fifty years old. It affects women more often than men, and is found present in young children.

Just heart breaking, isn't it?!

On average, there are over 6,000 Australians living with Scleroderma[1].

Most common Symptoms (cases will vary depending on which parts of the body have been affected):

- Changes in fingers and hands—hardening and tightening of the skin, puffiness. Skin may also appear shiny

1   https://www.sclerodermaaustralia.com.au/wp-content/uploads/2020/05/Scleroderma-Australia-Understanding-and-Managing-Scleroderma-Ed5.pdf

- Blood vessels—fingers change colour in response to cold temperatures and stress Fingers may also become extremely numb and cause discomfort and pain

- Swelling in the wrists, knees, and ankles—inflammation built-up

- Red spots on the face, hands and chest

- Problems with the digestive system—severe acid reflux which may damage the oesophagus

- Calcium deposits under the skin

There is no specific test for scleroderma to reach a diagnosis but a series of tests, physical examinations and biopsies can determine if you have scleroderma and what type.

There are two types of classes for scleroderma. Localised scleroderma is very mild and affects some parts of the skin, whereas Systemic Sclerosis (could be either Limited—referred to as CREST syndrome or Diffuse—more serious complications, affects the internal organs and characterised as fatal) is most severe and considered life threatening.

Crest Syndrome refers to 5 features: Calcinosis, Raynaud's, Oesophagus leads to difficulty swallowing, Sclerodactyly—thickening and tightening of the skin caused by excess collagen and Telangiectasia—red spots on the hands and face

It is common to have Raynaud's with Scleroderma. There are certain drugs to help manage the cold sensation and numbness feeling in the fingers, toes and help to increase restriction of blood flow associated with the phenomenon. It is also common to develop painful sores on the fingertips and ulcers.

The severity of each symptom is treated individually. Treatments used help to improve symptoms to a certain degree.

I continued to roam the internet for information and encountered many worst-case scenarios and some good recovery stories. I was literally in "PANIC" mode. I had to explore the short and long-term expectations of the disease, educate myself and take proactive steps to keep well and do what I can to stay alive.

There is ongoing research to determine what triggers the body to produce too much inflammation and excessive collagen. People are working hard to raise awareness and find a cure. There are a variety of online channels and face-to-face support groups to help people connect with others facing similar challenges. Like many support groups, they provide different types of help to the wounded and for their family and friends.

I had plans for how I wished to live my life, and now they were crumbling right before my eyes. This was not supposed to be happening to me. This was not part of my plan... I had a career, I had just purchased my first home, and I had just become an aunty. I had bigger goals, to get married and start a family. I wanted to travel. How could I come to terms with this disease? I was not sure what to expect, but I knew it was going to be a rough and long journey ahead.

It is a disease that would quickly change my life forever, slowly turn me into stone, and was something beyond my control. It was very unsettling. My future looked bleak.

My journey with scleroderma begins...

PART 2: LIVING WITH SCLERODERMA

MY LIFE PUSHED on as normal until late November 2013 when I developed inflammation of the skin in my hands, legs, and arms. My skin was getting really tight, I was struggling to bend my wrists; it was so hard for me to walk in heels, there were times I would wrap my wrists with bandages just to ease the pain. I had also developed several digital ulcers on my fingertips and elbows; they were extremely painful.

I remember I was on my way to work; the train pulled up at the station, I hopped off the train and headed to the office. It's almost a six-minute walk from the station to the office, but I felt light-headed that morning and I had this urge to vomit. My legs were aching, feeling weak and shaky. I looked down at my ankles and they were swollen. I had the swollen ankles of a pregnant woman. I could barely walk, I leaned against the brick wall for support as commuters walked past me to their offices and some made eye contact with me. It was at that moment I needed someone just to pick me up and carry me to the office.

As time progressed, my condition continued to get worse. My weight had dropped a few kilos and I would experience shortness of breath walking short distances. I was not exercising, but I knew something was wrong. A visit to my local rheumatologist detected crackling sounds in my right lung and sclerotic changes in my chest and abdominal wall. I saw physical changes in my body that I was certainly not prepared for.

The rheumatologist prescribed a drug called Methotrexate to help slow down the progression of the disease. Methotrexate is a chemotherapy and immune suppressive agent used to effectively treat rheumatoid arthritis, autoimmune diseases, cancer, and other types of immune disorders. The most common side effects are nausea, diarrhoea, mouth ulcers, dry skin, tiredness, headaches, weight loss and confusion.

For the next six months, every Sunday morning I would inject a fine needle of 12.5mg of methotrexate (yellow liquid) into fatty layer under my skin at a 90-degree angle. I found the whole injecting process to be really painful. I hated needles, and the pain associated with it! When the hard part was finally over, I would sit in my room with my thoughts and cry softly so no one could hear me in the other room. I would often hide my emotions to keep the image that I am a strong and stable type, and not appear so vulnerable to others. It just seemed a lot easier hiding my emotions. Scleroderma had just become my enemy.

> *It hurts, I cry, I take one day at a time. It's painful. It's uncomfortable. You don't own me. Living with uncertainty, limitations, and complications. Each day is different, it's exhausting but I am smiling, I AM FINE.... Scleroderma does NOT define who I am.*

By the year of 2014, my symptoms had progressed. Whilst I was still working and travelling back and forth via train, my body was quickly deteriorating. The year bought more treatments and tests. I had minor issues with my oesophagus swallowing food, many sleepless nights, and I was plagued with negative thoughts. I had muscle soreness, inflammation and pain in my joints and mild shortness of breath, just a few things of many. Some areas of my body become very stiff and to my disappointment I could no longer walk in high heels or walk long distances. My ankles were stiff, I was losing flexibility, but my range of motion was intact.

One afternoon I was on the train home from work as the train approached my station, I got up to walk down the stairs when I lost control of both knees and I tumbled forward. I landed on my hip, bruised my knees and shoulder. Two passengers on the train witnessed the fall and quickly came to my aid. They held me up as I brushed off the dirt from my hands and knees, and asked me if I was okay. I was so embarrassed about the fall, but angry and hurt by what was happening to me that I cried the whole way home.

I was trying so hard to keep it together.

My pain won't stop, this physical, emotional and mental cruelty on my body, it is constant. Every day is a battle. Why me? This is not fair. I can't live my life like this…

I am no longer in control of my body.

Methotrexate was certainly not working. The rheumatologist had increased the dosage, but scleroderma was still progressing. I was starting to lose hope. Blood tests confirmed no improvements with my skin. I was so scared of experimenting with further treatment that would cause more damage to immune system. Whilst searching for new rheumatologist to seek a second opinion, I made some temporary adjustments to my diet and lifestyle to help me deal with my symptoms in the short term. I had a pharmacy of drugs to manage my symptoms.

After days of researching, I finally came across a well-known rheumatologist Dr Christopher Browne based Sydney who specialises in scleroderma. My first consultation with the specialist was not my best experience; I received the news that I would need a bone marrow transplant, also known as (Autologous HSCT—Hematopoietic Stem Cell Transplant). My mother and I had very little knowledge of this treatment, but after a very long discussion with the rheumatologist we understood the pros and cons of Stem Cell Transplant.

The specialist had supportive data, case studies that support the stem cell study and found survival rates and quality of life had improved for patients suffering from severe scleroderma.

I came to realise Methotrexate could not slow the progression of disease, so I immediately ceased it. I was back in Dr Browne's office, my skin had thickened in most parts of my body, I was extremely fatigued, and constantly out of breath. My lungs were not expanding. Tests later confirmed I had developed some scarring tissue around the lungs, my lungs are slowly becoming stiff. The rheumatologist was very persistent to get me on the Stem Cell Transplant program, calling me frequently as I was viable and suitable candidate for this trial and they were likely to see good results. The Stem Cell Transplant could reverse my condition and improve my quality of life, but it was not a simple decision for me to make, it was rather a difficult and emotional one.

All I could do was cry; there were so many things to consider… what if chemotherapy failed? The emotional shock of having to re-evaluate my life priorities and face the possibility of death lingered in the back of my mind. I knew the transplant was my only chance of survival… but I was not ready to take that risk.

At this point I was still working full time and carried on with my work duties, but I found it very hard for me to concentrate on my job and missed deadlines. I wasn't sleeping well and very irritable, had this burning sensation in my body and constant pain in my fingers and sores at the tip of my fingers made it difficult for me to use the keyboard to type. I wasn't sure what would happen to me, but I was scared of losing my independence to Scleroderma. I was passionate and driven with goals, but suffered from a sense of overwhelming emotion with the fear of losing myself, the wholeness that presents who I am. I had a hard time adjusting to the pain, and there was nothing I could do to relieve it.

As weeks progressed, my fatigue was gradually getting worse, my legs felt heavy, my arms were stiff and sore, but that didn't stop me. I would get out of bed at 5am, get ready for work and be in the office by 8am. I was determined to outlive this disease. I just had to keep up the appearance, makeup, hair and outfit, even if I was crying on the inside.

I was not prepared to die just yet. I prayed religiously day and night to God (Allah) to ease my pain and give me the strength I needed through this difficult time.... I needed a sign, something to work with, I was seeking reassurance, just some form of validation that I was going to be okay and everything will be fine. I was scared and anxious about my health and what my future looked like, did I have a future? Would I get my happy ending?

In spite of it all, I had the love and support of family and friends at my side, but this was not enough to ease my mind. The doctor said I had five months to live, my body was suffering a quick process of deterioration. I was quickly learning what death looks like, but my mind could simply not accommodate this weakness. I could not accept this was my fate.

I was starting to lose my faith in Allah, my prayers were not being answered. I was so angry. Why wasn't he helping? Or healing me? Here I was suffering, and only Allah could ease my pain and make it all go away. I was calling out to him day and night; I had so many questions for him. *Why is this happening to me? What did I do wrong? I am a good person and you know this, so why am I being punished?* I was trying so hard to maintain a positive attitude, but I felt depressed, and I had never been the depressive type.

I took it upon myself to read about the Stem Cell Transplant; the risks involved, shared my insights and thoughts with family, and consulted the opinion of a very close family doctor. But I wasn't mentally ready to participate in this clinical trial and declined the offer. Dr Browne explained that the procedure was not a cure but it would help to improve my quality of life and could reverse my condition by 50%. The success rate was excellent; the study is also been conducted in other hospitals around Australia, Europe and USA to help others like myself suffering from auto-immune disorders. The transplant involves eliminating the 'bad cells' from the body using chemotherapy and replacing them with 'good healthy cells' that are collected during the stem cell process.

I am functional, but I am not disabled. I am in chronic pain, my body has betrayed me.... but I am a fighter.

In the last year or so, I have seen my body and hands change quite significantly. By the end of 2014—early 2015, my body had deteriorated very quickly, my breathing was irregular. There were so many warnings signs. The autoimmune disease was destroying my immune system, and it was becoming much harder for me to ignore....

I was back in Dr Browne's office. My Raynaud's had been playing up for most of the time, and the opened ulcers on my fingers and elbows were extremely sore and painful.

My knees were unstable and often buckled. It would happen so unexpectedly, my knees would give away and with no warning I would stumble and fall. The second time my knees gave out, I was on the train home again. I just got on the train and I was walking down the stairs holding on to the railing, but my knees buckled in and I fell forward. I was so embarrassed, with so many people staring at me I as struggled to lift myself from the floor. I finally managed to get up, and found a seat. I sobbed quietly in my seat as tears rolled down my face.

My struggle with scleroderma was causing my family an immense amount of heartache. I tried so hard to hide my emotions, I didn't want to express how I was feeling and what I was thinking, but my family could see right through me.

As close as we have always been with my father, I've never seen him express any emotion, but the first time I saw him cry was when his mother and father passed away, and the second was when I got diagnosed with Scleroderma. Mum was always emotional, she would look at me and start crying and move to the other room.

I had very little energy to go to work; I struggled to get out of bed and I was always calling in sick. It was impossible for me to manage my energy levels whilst living with a chronic illness. Some days, despite the pain, I would get out of bed and make my way to the office. When I was in the office working, I would be sitting at my desk feeling exhausted. I struggled to hold my arms out straight. I had trouble lifting my arms over my shoulders. I endured so many sleepless nights. Everyday activities exhausted me. I could no longer squat on the floor, picking myself up from the floor was not as simple but progressively harder. My ability to use my hands, arms and knees for help were intact. I needed that elevated push, but it was all too difficult. I could no longer tie my hair up in a ponytail or tie my shoelaces. By this stage, my body was producing too much collagen and the blood vessels were no longer working properly, causing stiffness and pain in the joints and muscles, I could no longer bare rings. All I could do was cry.

This one time I got off the train and walked over to the escalators when I heard the following announcements, 'the lifts are out of order and the escalators near the station master office are temporary unavailable.' Commuters were told to take the stairs. I stood helplessly at the bottom, looking up at all those stairs. It was one of the worst things that could ever happen to me. My biggest struggle was how I would make it up those stairs with all these people rushing behind me to get to the office. My heart was pounding so hard and I had this intense fear inside of me. I felt like I was in danger or something; I was experiencing hot flushes. It was impossible for me to climb those stairs when my hip, knee caps and ankles ached. I realised I was having a panic attack. I was trying desperately to remain calm. I took my first step walking up the stairs but at a slow pace regardless of those behind me. When I finally reached the top of the stairs, I burst into tears. I was relieved and exhausted at the same time. It was at that moment I wished I was dead. Even the simplest act of walking had become a difficult and frightening task for me.

I am bent and broken. I am damaged. I am angry and hurting. I will never escape this pain.

Scleroderma, you stole my body and tormented me in so many ways. You have drained the life out of me and for that I HATE YOU. I am so exhausted from trying to keep it together.... I wish I could just stop breathing... and be laid to rest.

Towards the end, Dad would carry me between appointments. I could no longer walk.

I was powerless. I was at the lowest point in my life battling a vicious disease. No one could understand or relate to my pain or struggle, my life was just unbearable. It soon became a rather simple decision to have the transplant, taking the risk to improve my quality of life.

There are so many things that scleroderma took away from me—I used to have tons of energy, but it was now impossible for me to live a normal life. I missed out on birthdays, weddings and social gatherings and all other social activities. For the majority of the time, I just kept to myself. It was very difficult for me to face my extended family and friends. I would accept invitations but cancel at the last minute. This cruel disease had cost me relationships, friendships, my career, restricted my ability to go places and do things I would normally do.

I also went through self-pity phase; I had very little control over what was happening to me. It was so difficult for me to accept this life, stuff like this was NOT supposed to happen to me. I had my whole life mapped out... Now I was in this depressed state. My life was crumbling and all I could do was watch it fall apart. Negative emotions overwhelmed me.

For a long time, I'd been trying so hard to stay calm, be strong and think positive thoughts. It was almost impossible for me to overcome this terrible state, I would never be better again. It was a big shock. I was feeling utterly helpless and my sadness became unbearable. Feeling sorry for myself was self-destructive, but safe and easy to do. Everything seemed to be going wrong, it was only natural for me to feel this way. It was tough, but I had valid reasons. I wallowed in my misery and self-loathing; I could no longer bear the pain and suffering anymore. In the midst of it all, I lost my sense of worth, value and self-esteem.

Even the loving support from my family was not enough to lift my spirits from this self–pity phase. I continued to dwell on what was happening to me and cry endlessly. The worst part of it all, I have a clock buzzing annoyingly over my head.

I was so angry with everyone that stood in my way. Avoiding my friends and extended family seemed like the right thing to do at the time. Let's face it, I couldn't deal with their happy and eventful lives, while mine was falling apart. I didn't feel guilty about avoiding them either. I was feeling resentful, girls my age were enjoying life, some were getting married, some travelling and here I was trying to decide if I should proceed with the stem cell transplant or not. There were so many things I was missing out on. All I wanted to do was hide and stay away from those living a good healthy life. I envied them; I was jealous. I felt a sense of betrayal!

My body and face were changing; suddenly everything was changing for the worse. I could no longer look at myself in the mirror. Every day there was something new to deal with. The struggle with scleroderma was so real.

Life was unfair. Being vulnerable is not easy, but I wasn't ready to share my painful experiences of Scleroderma to my family and friends… It was a painful period, and my self-hatred just got worse. I was trying so hard to act tough, like I am in control of this condition, but I certainly was NOT. When I was alone, I would break down and cry. I was always putting on a good front. It was my way of dealing with the difficult situation. I HATED BEING SICK.

How was I going to survive this transplant? I had stomached every possible treatment, and they all failed me. My fear of death, the idea haunted me. How could life end so suddenly? It was freaking me out. To leave my old life behind and start a new life, it would take time to adjust. I had to accept the harsh reality I would never be my old self again. This treatment could either kill me or give me another ten to thirty years to live. I was not happy that my life was changing, but I had to help myself. I had to shift my focus of what was really important here, 'my quality of life'.

It was also a very confusing and painful time for my family. I owed it to them to stop feeling sorry for myself and explore all options to outlive this disease. I decided to go ahead with the transplant. I had to change the course of my path and my attitude to life.

I am trying to be strong and fearless. I laugh, smile and pretend to be happy, but I doubt myself. I am scared, and I remain torn.

Mum was very confused and total denial of what was happening to me. She couldn't accept how sick I was and that the Stem Cell Treatment is my only chance of survival. It hurt me to see her in so much pain. Mum was so sure this phase would pass and I'd be back to my old self again. She was scared and grieving at how this vicious disease had robbed me of a normal life. My illness was causing a rip between my family, they were all so distressed. The old Claudia was gone, and she was not coming back. I went from a fun, happy, career focussed independent woman, to become a young woman who spends so much of her time in bed suffering from severe chronic pain. *She is unable to perform the simplest tasks because she cannot physically move anymore. Sitting, standing or laying down flat on her back, everything hurts and it's all she thinks about before she sleeps and when she wakes up. There is no turn off pain signal. It was a life sentence. Her bed has suddenly become her new prison in her home.* The disheartening reality was that scleroderma was turning me into stone and was destroying my body and soul, something of which I simply had no control of. My family was terribly afraid of losing me. They were all trying so hard to keep it together, but mum was an emotional mess. Seeing them all in pain sadden me deeply.

We held a family meeting to discuss the Stem Cell Transplant. Mum shared her opinion and expressed her concerns about the treatment, but my father and siblings objected. They all agreed it was the best for me to proceed with the Stem Cell transplant. I walked over to my mother and wrapped my arms around her waist as I held on to her tightly. I had to reassure her that everything would be ok and not to be afraid. It was no secret she was hurting and feared the unexpected. My father and siblings were keen to pack my bags and send me to the hospital to begin treatment immediately. Mum was extremely annoyed at how encouraging, persuasive and supportive my siblings were about the clinical trial.

However, it was important for me to acknowledge the emotional impact this was having on my family, so we talked about our feelings and I was very up front about mine too. We also discussed the pros and cons of the transplant, giving each other time to digest this information. Mum was finally on board, but it took a lot of convincing and encouragement. I found myself smiling and crying at the same time. These amazing people I call my family, they fill my heart with so much love and joy. I constantly remind myself of how blessed I am to have them in my life. They are my inspiration, comfort, happy, safe place and support system. The love of a family is the greatest gift of all.

My family who accepts me for who I am, that would do everything and anything to see smile and be happy again. To be my old joyful self. The love of family and bond we have is like no other. Unconditional love. Our bond, faith and love—we stick together, we are family.

The clinical trial is run by St Vincent's Hospital under the care of Haematologist Dr John Moore and Rheumatologist Helen Englert. My parents and I met with Dr John Moore. During the consultation process he explained the risks and benefits involved in the experiment, and how the data collected would be used for further research. Once I agreed to participate in the trial, the haematologist made me sign a fifteen page consent form.

The following day I resigned from my job, for good reasons. I was lost to my battle to Scleroderma. I had no energy. I was always calling in sick, but when I wasn't calling in sick, I was pretending I could do it all. I didn't want to listen to my parent's advice about quitting my job to help improve my health. I would go to work despite being chronically ill, performing to the best of my ability, but at the same time my insides were hurting. All I really wanted to do was lay down on the office floor, curl up and sob quietly.

I spent so much time trying to be perfect and doing my best; I lost focus of what was really important here, my HEALTH.

Scleroderma changes people, it changed me. The smallest things are now much more appreciated, it is a continuous fight, I can't ignore and avoid you. You nasty disease.

Prior to treatment there were some things I had to do before I could spend time in hospital. It was important for me to take care of loose ends and ensure my financial affairs were in order. I made arrangements with my solicitor to inform my family of my will in the event that I didn't survive the transplant. All this was necessary so I could focus on the transplant with a clear-mind.

Preparing myself for treatment caused me some anxiety and worry. I was certainly not prepared for what was yet to come. I had trouble sleeping, because I was thinking of all the worst possible things that I could encounter during the transplant. I made myself sick in the stomach.

Leading up to the transplant I spent most of the time laying on the couch in front of the heater, I was always cold. I could barely move, I had restricted mobility, and I was extremely fatigued. I felt defeated. On the home front, things were not good either. It was an emotional and difficult time for my family, but they went to great lengths to hide their emotions and cheer me up.

Mum would care for me in hospital. She would spend all her days couped up with me in the hospital ward and the rest of the family would come to visit me on the weekends. It was a full-time job that was mentally and physically exhausting.

The hospital organised affordable and comfortable accommodation for my family because we lived so far from the hospital. This was helpful for my family so they could keep a close eye on me and monitor my progress, so when dad came up during the week mum and dad would stay in the accommodation provided.

My life was full of uncertainty; so many twists and turns. All I could do was wait for the pieces to come together. Life was insisting I take this route. Would it be possible for me to return home after the transplant? Was I unbreakable?

Uncertainty the whole way.

Anxious. Don't judge my insecurities, I am a confused girl.

Doubt float and heart is quiet, reserved and cold. Nowhere to run.

Worry, pain and fear day by day. Her heart mourns the body that has betrayed her.

I have nothing left but Allah.

PART 3: PRE- STEM CELL TRANSPLANT – PLANNING PHASE

A QUICK OVERVIEW…

An Autologous Stem Cell Transplant requires collecting one's healthy blood cells, which are then frozen for later use. The remaining existing blood cells are destroyed with high doses of chemotherapy. Two weeks later, the frozen stem cells that were collected are reinfused back into the body to replace the stem cells that were destroyed and produce healthy new stem cells.

We left the haematologist's office with an officially set date. The transplant would take place on 23rd September 2015. Before I could commence with the treatment, I had to complete a number of tests that were mandatory for the clinical trial. These tests include HRCT, CT scans, chest x-rays, EKG, lung function test, urine tests and blood work. The tests would determine if my body was fit enough for the transplant and safe to proceed with treatment.

I was feeling anxious that my admission was only two sleeps away. On the 23rd September 2015 I was admitted into St Vincent's Hospital. Prior to the transplant, a central venous catheter was placed in a large vein of my neck, which connects to the chest. The catheter is a long narrow tube which is made up of two ports that hang out of the skin. These ports are used to draw blood, administer chemotherapy, blood transfusions and other medications. The procedure takes roughly thirty minutes; the central line is surgically inserted with a local anaesthetic. Having the catheter in my neck was very unpleasant and painful experience. It was very uncomfortable. The ports are flushed out daily to keep them open so fluids will flow in smoothly.

A central line was also inserted into my right arm, with only one port to draw out blood and to administer other drugs painlessly.

Transplant Protocol:

The days leading up to the Stem Cell Transplant are negative days, anything after 'Transfusion DAY 0' are all plus positive days.

Pre- stem cell timeline is made up into 7-9 days

<u>Day 1:</u> Dosages of Cyclophosphamide (chemotherapy) is infused in one of the lines of the catheter for the next five to seven days. This is commonly unknown as the conditioning therapy.

<u>Day2:</u> Filgastim 10mcg (which is used to stimulate stem cell growth) is injected under my skin for the next seven days.

<u>Day9:</u> I am wheeled from St Vincent's Hospital to Kinghorn Cancer Clinic (a five-minute walk between the buildings) in a wheelchair to have my stem cells collected, a process called Leukophersis.

The head nurse inserted a needle/drip into each arm. For the next nine hours a machine would draw out blood, collecting the stem cells, and returning the blood cells back into the body. It is a continuous cycle.

I was exhausted, my muscles were aching, I was falling in and out of sleep mode, I was hungry and very thirsty but I was trying to avoid fluids so I wouldn't have to use the bathroom, or we would have to stop the procedure and repeat the cycle from the beginning. When enough stem cells have been collected, I am wheeled back to St Vincent's Hospital for more doses of chemotherapy.

Stem Cell Infusion 'Day 0' is scheduled two weeks away, the big day when I will receive my stem cells back.

Transplant Phase–Conditioning Therapy

For the next two weeks, four doses of Chemotherapy along with four doses of Antithymiocyte Globin (ATG) are infused into the ports of the catheter in my neck (cycles known as -6 to -2 days). ATG is used to help suppress the immune system so the collected blood cells will grow and develop into a healthy immune system, when infused back into the body.

The most common side effects with chemotherapy can range anywhere from mild to severe. My chemotherapy experience was intense, it really slowed me down, and I was incredibly weak and tired. I could barely get out of bed but I had to be strong for my family.

Nausea, vomiting, diarrhoea and weight loss

I struggled with a lot with nausea. It was a constant struggle to eat without vomiting. I would vomit at the sight or smell of food, during and after meals. I could not keep anything down. My stomach was upset all the time. My body frame was shrinking; I was becoming invisible and small.

My haematologist doctor prescribed an anti-nausea medication to reduce the vomiting. I was extremely dehydrated and my mouth was really dry. I was constantly drinking water, trying to keep up with my fluids and sucking on ice cubes.

Hair loss

My hair is a large part of my identity and self-esteem, it defines my strength and character. I had long dark brown thick hair prior to the chemotherapy and cut it short, knowing that I'd be losing my hair over the next few weeks. One morning I woke up to find my hair all over my pillow and hair on the shower floor. It was hard for me to accept that I was losing my hair. Losing my hair has been a devastating and frightening experience to my self-image and emotional well-being. My hair mattered, it reflects my personality, what mood I am in, how I desire others to perceive me, what kind person I am. So you can understand now why I was sad and feeling so vulnerable; I really felt as though I really lost a sense of myself and my identity. It was one of the worst things about chemotherapy; no one wants to lose their hair.

The next morning, I was sitting in a hair salon ready to shave it all off. I honestly thought I was mentally and emotionally prepared for this, but I certainly wasn't. I began obsessing about how long it would take for my hair to grow back again. The shock of my baldness was painful and embarrassing. I felt less of a woman because I had lost my hair and I didn't recognise the woman staring back at me. Soon after, I lost all my eyelashes.

I lost my IDENTITY. I look at my old photos and I miss my old self, but I remind myself she no longer exists. I hate the camera. The day came and you stole my beauty.

The emotional burden keeps piling up. Scleroderma I HATE YOU.

Heart rate, Fever and Insomnia

I had a heart rate of 165 and a fever of 41. Most of my days were spent in bed, not much to do but just sleep, pray and read. I had very little energy; I was drowsy and worn out. Some days I was just so cold, I'll ask the nurse for extra blankets. There were some nights I would lay awake living the feeling I was so close to death. I had difficulty breathing, tight chest pain with some chemotherapy fluid built up around heart.

Tiredness, stress and anxiety

I was extremely fatigued and exhausted, feeling utterly helpless. The chemotherapy made me horribly sick in the stomach. My limbs were sore, I had muscular pain and throbbing headaches. I found it difficult to do daily activities such as getting out of bed or having a shower without support.

I was quite anxious and nervous about this life-changing experience, and I wasn't sure if I would be getting better anytime soon. I couldn't wait for this phase in my life to pass. I wanted to be my old self again, free of this illness. How was I able to return to my old life when I was broken? I could never be carefree and live an ordinary life.

Infertility

The mourning process of losing my hair did not compare to the one of the most devastating news of all — premature menopause and infertility. The doctor had warned me there would be some changes to my body after the chemotherapy treatment. I hate my menopausal body. I didn't realise how intense these symptoms were.

Chemotherapy causes infertility, so my chances of falling pregnant are very slim. The option to freeze my eggs was too late, timing had been an issue.

Today I am a 36 years old woman mourning the loss that I may never be able to conceive a child. I am utterly devastated at not being able to have a child of my own. I lost my chance of being a mother and grandmother. How do you get over something like this? You don't. That's the sad and true reality. It's tragic and an unfortunate life-changing experience.

Not being a mother has scarred me for life, and that's something I have to live with. Do I really think I'll end up having a miracle baby? I don't know anymore. I feel a deep, profound feeling of loss, this emptiness encountered. This is certainly not how I planned to live my life. Will I ever be called mum?

I could sit here and cry for hours, I have no else to blame but myself… My life could have been different.

Then I reminded myself I needed to survive this transplant, so I blocked out the empty feeling in my heart and mentally focused on getting through the transplant.

Isolation

I was moved into isolation because my body was at risk of infections. I had my own room in the hospital ward with a window view of Sydney Centre Point Tower.

The isolation took a toll on my sense of well-being and my

mental state. I was sad and lonely. I was separated from the people I love when I needed them the most. I hated being alone and so disconnected from the world. I was constantly reminding myself there were so many things in my life that were worth fighting for, and I had to keep pushing forward and trust that it will all come together. I had to walk this rocky and painful road to recreate myself again. My time in isolation gave me an opportunity to reflect back on my journey, appreciate it for what it is, change the way I think and feel and learn to become much more positive person. From my standing point, I had to accept what has happened to me and the seriousness of my illness, although I wasn't comfortable with it. So I told myself, this is your life, accept the experience as it is. Although I desperately wanted to resist this fact, I couldn't ignore it anymore. I needed to accept it more willingly and wholeheartedly. I accepted the challenge life had thrown at me with so any uncertainties and inconsistencies and consequences that I may not always get my way. I owed it to myself and my family to fight this battle and learn to navigate through negativity, accepting with grace whatever shape or form. I would push through the hard times by putting on a brave face and smiling with my 'can-do' attitude. I've realised how far I have come and I smile because I am truly proud of myself.

PART 4: THE TRANSPLANT (STEM CELL INFUSION) – DAY 0 'SECOND BIRTHDAY'

A new day, new beginnings, new hope, a new chapter for a fresh new start.

THEN IT HAPPENED, the big day arrived, September 30th 2015.

DAY 0 I was excited and nervous at the same time. The blood stem cells that were collected and regenerated were infused into one of the ports of the catheter in my neck. These new baby cells enter the body and make their way to the bone marrow, where they begin to grow and rebuild the immune system. The sensation is cold and overwhelming. At this point, I am afraid something will go wrong. Just thinking about my own death gives me the creeps, the intense feeling of anxiety, fear and rage.

During this time, my immune system is highly comprised. So daily blood works are required to see if the bone marrow is generating any new cells. Blood was drawn from the cannula in my arm. Daily tests monitor my heart rate, kidney and liver function, which are standard. My weight is also observed along with vital signs such as temperature, pulse and blood pressure.

While the stem cells were slowly formulating and redeveloping the new immune system, my red cells (carry oxygen around the body) and white cells (fight off infections) drop, which was totally expected. For the first week, a nurse would inject a drug under the skin of my stomach to help generate the growth of white cells in my bone marrow. The following day my platelets (cells that form clots to stop bleeding and bruising) dropped, and I had to receive an infusion of platelets via catheter.

I had very little control over what was happening to me, in a flash my entire life had changed. In theory, this was the end of my old life, as I lay in bed glancing out the window trying to imagine what life I could have lived if I didn't get sick or how my future would look. But none of that mattered anymore, neither did it make any sense. My life and lifelong goals were all suddenly altered by my illness, and it soon became impossible for me to return to normal again. My normal suddenly became new normal dealing with health challenges. My thoughts were interrupted by a nurse wanting to check blood pressure. Suddenly I was back into my war zone, tackling one more battle at a time.

I also encountered two sets of red blood transfusions for the bone marrow to start working properly. I felt horribly sick in the stomach. My ongoing fevers would trigger hot and cold shivers, my muscles were sore and they ached. I felt miserable. I felt utterly helpless and experienced prolonged feelings of hopeless and sadness.

By the second week, my blood counts had improved, and I was slowly getting better. I was able to get out of bed, walk around my room, stretch my legs and walk to the bathroom. It was still diffi-cult for me to consume food. I was still on anti-nausea medications to reduce vomiting. I always ate in small portions, it was hard to gain weight.

Although I felt powerless in my current state, I was relieved that I managed to get this far. I was still alive and trying to see a dif-ferent perspective of this new version of my life. That being said, I remained fragile and exhausted.

My poor mother witnessed my pain and suffering, along with the discomfort and fear, just to stay alive. Mum stood helplessly watch-ing as my heart rate and temperature soared. There was a late night visit to the operating room to replace the infected central line in my neck and arm that were itchy and very painful. The doctor exam-ined the central lines and instructed the nurse to take both them out. Both central lines are replaced, but the cannula in my arm soon became a blood clot. At 2am in the morning, the doctor hooked me up to Electrocardiogram machine to measure the electrical activity of my heart, to understand why I am experiencing some mild chest pain and having difficulty breathing.

The pain won't go away. I want to scream, but I cry helplessly into my mother's arms. The pain never leaves me. My job is to

*stay alive, but why is it so hard? I am so damn strong, but why
do I feel so weak? I wish I was dead. This disease is a curse.*

I spent nights looking outside my bedroom window of the hospital ward. The city office building's lights were lit up and were so beautiful, the city looked so alive. Even the city streets glowed as people moved between the glimmers heading to their destination wherever that may be as heavy traffic moved in both directions. Meanwhile, in the hospital ward sounds of the monitors continuously beeped, nurses moved between room to room checking in on patients and the cries of a young man lingered between the walls of the corridor. In the next room, a man in his early 30s was dying from stage four cancer. The experience was unsettling. I looked at my phone and it was 11pm. In the dark hour of the night, the man wept into his pillow in pain and I cried helplessly for the unknown man in the next room. His cries were silenced and I finally stopped crying. The emotions of this man seemed to have affected me, I wanted to comfort him, to give him some hope that everything would be okay but then again, I wasn't sure of that either. I felt so torn and upset for this man, sadness filled me and there was little I could do but say a prayer for him asking Allah to ease his pain and suffering.

When I woke the next morning, he was gone....

I woke up with the sunshine in my eyes. The hospital ward was quiet. No cries lingered in the hallways and I sat upright in bed, waiting for a nurse to respond to my call bell. At this point I was sitting at the edge of my bed with my fluffy pink robe on. One of the nurses from the night shift walked in, high on caffeine, trying to fight the fatigue. She reached for the blood pressure machine to check my vital signs and wanted to know why I was up so early. I asked her questions about the man next door and if I could go see to him. To my disappointment, he was discharged from hospital. Given that he has stage four cancer, his internal organs were damaged and the clinical trial was not safe for his condition. His family decided to seek treatment elsewhere. I believe he travelled to Germany to participate in one of their advanced trials but died a week later after treatment.

I walked past his room; the bed was empty. The bed sheets were being replaced by one of the nurses and a janitor was cleaning the bathroom. The day before I could hear the sobs of a man in pain, today I was staring hard at the empty bed. The thought really affected me. I was certainly unprepared for what was to follow. I had a hard time accepting this man's death. A stranger that had no connection to me whatsoever, but the sound of his cry rests in my ears, a memory I will never let go of. I am mourning the death of a stranger. I felt a deeper personal loss. I was overwhelmed by shock and grief. Strangely enough, I felt like my soul connected with his; I felt deeper connection to this tragedy. I couldn't believe he was gone. I was grieving from afar. I was heartbroken for his family to be suffering such an immeasurable loss.

As the days went by, I put on my energy and focus on Allah. Praying for the remedies of all my pain to go away. I had confidence that Allah would ease my pain and suffering, to protect me in this lifetime on earth. I had a new deeper appreciation for my Islam religion. I had no hesitation admitting I was a Muslim, and I was proud of it. I feel that in this present moment Allah has opened up my heart to spirituality and I will not turn my back on him regardless of difficult life gets. Personally, I feel a sense of gratitude and inspired for what is yet to become. I am blessed for the strength, courage and determination he has empowered over me to get me through these dark hours of my life. I have led a good life and I feel I am being rewarded, Allah chose me because he loves me. He has bestowed patience in my heart; he is my saviour.

Ya rab (you Allah) I trust that you will keep me safe. I trust that you will protect me as I am loyal to you. I trust that you will inspire me to be the better version of myself. I trust that you will give me the energy and passion to live the life I deserve. I trust that you will bring joy and laughter into my life. I trust that you will help me find happiness. I trust that you will guide me when life gets tough. I trust that you will make me whole again and shower me with peace and comfort. I trust you even when I don't hear from you, ya rab you are most gracious and merciful of all.

My journey in hospital continued for another two weeks, but I really wanted to go home, I was confined to my hospital bed for so long. Someone days I'd wake up feeling good and the next day my body was too exhausted and needed rest. The stem cell transplant was done, I wanted to recover quickly but I could not let this emotional pain hold me down. Mum was there to constantly remind me that this was for just for a short time and I would be back on my feet soon again. I missed my dad, brothers and sister, but the road to home seemed so far. I was homesick.

Mum's presence helped me to push forward. She made things easier and smoother for me. But I depended on mum for everything from bathing me to preparing homemade meals. I disliked the hospital food, which added to my nausea. I would lay awake at night watching mum as she prayed helplessly with her eyes closed and Lebanese beads in her hands. I could feel she was physically, mentally and emotionally exhausted, but she refused to give up on me. The love of mother is like no other. She helped pull me through at my worst and finally came to terms with what I was happening to me.She encouraged me to take one day at a time and not to think about tomorrow. We also prayed together, she would read chapters from the Holy Quran as I was drifted off to sleep. Hearing mum's voice, those holy words was very comforting and reassuring.

What does my life mean to me? I am slowly coming to terms that death is not my answer or escape plan. I want to die when it's my time, which is not definitely not now. I no longer fear death. My time on earth remains.

Life simply needs to go on and I need to move forward with this new version of my life.

Dear Mum,

First of all, I just want you to know how much I LOVE YOU. Can I just say... I am truly blessed to have you in my life. Because of you I am here today, you are my inspiration. Not only are you my mother but you also are my first love, best friend, my counsellor, teacher and my rock.

If it wasn't for your love, care and support, I would be completely lost without you. When I needed you, you were always there for me, so thank you mum. When I shared my deepest fears with you, you held me close and reassured me that it was going to be alright, and you were right. I found comfort on your shoulder, as I wept. You are my safe place. You helped me find my way when I was so restless and inpatient.

We held hands as we prayed together; you gave me the strength I needed to keep pushing forward. You are so not good at hiding your true feelings, you will laugh and smile but I felt your pain too mum. For every tear that you cried, I am sorry mum.

Thank you mum for putting up with me when I was in one of my unpredictable moods. I know I was very difficult and fought with you over useless things. For the times I pushed you away and caused you pain, I am truly sorry. I know you were trying so hard to do your best and keep it together.

You always found a way to make me laugh when I was in pain. You stayed with me in hospital for the entire treatment and never left my side. You slept on that old uncomfortable recliner chair, but you didn't care. You made me feel like I was at home. You even packed my favourite pillow, blanket and warm fluffy pink robe.

Looking back, how did you find the energy to be with me in hospital, then go home to cook, clean for me and my siblings? I admire your strength. You never ran out of energy. Mum, you are truly magnificent!

We fought this battle together right to the very end.

God blessed my siblings and I with an amazing person; so pure, beautiful face and soul. You are kind, honest, smart, caring, loving and compassionate person. I am so proud to call you my mother. I only hope that one day I can be just as amazing as you, I really do have big shoes to fill. I am so grateful and proud to be your daughter.

My siblings and I are very lucky to have a mother as strong, vibrant, and brave as you. Thank you for guiding me through this difficult phase of my life. I am forever grateful.

Lots of love,

Coco

PART 5: LEAVING THE HOSPITAL

———————————

My journey begins with the first step of leaving the hospital ward and all those familiar faces. My life could have ended so tragically, but Allah had other plans for me instead. I had no idea what the rest of the year would bring, but I had to navigate through these crossroads of life. I was exhausted, burnt out and but I needed to plan my journey of self-discovery, it's what I need to gain clarity of my new life.

I feel a sense of liberation.

I HAVE WAITED anxiously for this day to come. On the 15th October 2015, I was *FINALLY* discharged from St Vincent's Hospital, Sydney.

I was thrilled and blessed to have made it this far. My heart skipped a beat. I couldn't stop smiling. It was one of the happiest days of my life. I was going home. I am so overwhelmed with joy but frightened at the same time. The transition was going to be very difficult, but I was returning home to a safe environment, even with my limitations. I could still depend on my mother for support, but I also had to find ways to help myself and learn to adapt as I faced the new challenges in my life. It was time I got a hold of my life and stop being my own worst enemy.

I had a responsibility to look after my health and ensure I fully recovered from this transplant, so I could live a long and fulfilling life, but for now I was relieved that the treatment was finally over.

Before I could leave the hospital, the nurse removed the catheter from my neck and cannula in my arm. It felt good to be free of needles/tubes poking at me. I was given a bag with twenty-two different types of pills to take daily and a care plan checklist to follow for extra precautions. My final examination would determine if I was fit enough to go home:

- ✓ Blood cell counts are improving — platelets, red and white are steady

- ✓ No infections

- ✓ Nausea — vomiting has ceased or is controlled with medication

- ✓ Able to swallow medication

- ✓ Able to drink and eat

- ✓ No fever in the last 48 hours

✓ No bruising or bleeding in urine, gums, nose and bowel movements

✓ No diarrhoea, stomach aches or cramps

✓ No shortness of breath, cough, headache, severe pain, unexpected soreness

✓ No rash or itchy skin

✓ No blood clots around the central line and canella in the arm

Toolkit for selfcare checklist:

○ Follow the new diet plan of safe foods to eat

○ Drink plenty of fluids — only drink boiled water

○ Avoid pets

○ Avoid crowded places where there is risk of infections

○ Wear a medical face mask to help prevent infections

○ Ensure all medications are taken to reduce risk of infections

○ Shower regularly

○ Regular mouth care

○ Consistently wash hands

○ Gentle exercises

○ Avoid children that have exposure to chicken pox, measles and other viruses

○ No flowers in the bedroom or house

○ Keep visitors to a minimum for the first month or so

- Chemotherapy makes the skin very sensitive, avoid the sun as much as possible

- No smoking

All these tasks were achievable, and I was leaping in the right direction. Small steps = small victories, and this was my goal. It was something I could adhere too. This was my chance to turn my life around and have faith that it will all come together as Allah intended.

I rested for a few minutes on the edge of my hospital bed, and I looked around the place. I was feeling hopeful and relieved I've made this far; I was smiling that I had made peace with my pain. There were no uncomfortable feelings or 'what if' scenarios of something bad happening. Today was my last sleep in the hospital bed, no more noisy monitors, or nurses charging in at 2am in the morning to check my blood pressure or temperature, or the disgusting taste of hospital foods or that distinctive hospital smell that I dislike so much...

Now that I was returning home, I made a commitment to become the best version of myself, setting baby goals, an action plan... and seeing them through.

My path to self-discovery begins with self-awareness, my first step to self-improvement. I wrote a note to myself to see through the following;

- *Find acceptance*

- *Master my thoughts*

- *Find inner peace and happiness in the littlest things*

- *Stay focussed in good and bad situations*

- *Manage my emotions*

- *Set boundaries of my time and energy*

- ○ *Love myself again and accept my body issues*

- ○ *Work on my self-esteem issues and address my weaknesses*

- ○ *Build on my resilience*

PART 6: MY LONG JOURNEY HOME

———————

Family love, bond, safe happy place, memories, laughter and joy.
Circle of trust, love, and strength.
Home is where my heart is and where I belong…

THE TRANSITION AT home was unsettling and exhilarating at the same time. To be home was a blessing, but all my emotions came flooding back. Home is my safe place, but I had concerns about how I would cope with the ongoing challenges I faced. There were a number of precautions I had to take, one bad experience could comprise my immune system. My body needed time to recover from the emotional and physical effects of the transplant… Everything had changed and I needed a great deal of time to adjust to my new lifestyle. I was trying so hard to think positive and have an optimistic outlook; it was always hard to find my motivation to stay positive, but it was easier to shut off. I admit I had trouble sleeping; I was trying so hard to simplify my life; I lived with the constant fear that something bad may happen today, tonight tomorrow. I believed the negative self-talk in my head, instead of building better habits of self-talk. Focusing on my self-discovery plan all the time was exhausting and required a lot of hard work. I set too many individual goals and my focus and energy were slim to none. I was burnt out and overwhelmed, I was falling back into my old habits.

I wanted to bring my goals to life, reach my destination '*To be Normal again*' but instead of taking small little steps as I initially planned, I was taking giant leaps and hoping for the best…. *I had set myself up for failure and disappointment.*

I felt I was staring directly at a stop sign…

I have always shared a close bond with my siblings. Time at home with my siblings was exactly what I needed. It is comforting and very important for my mental health to not be alone. There was no pressure to talk about my feelings or the time I spent in the hospital, just being there with them was enough. I need that social interaction. Their presence acknowledges the support, love and comfort which I needed but I missed terribly.

My struggle with Scleroderma had strengthened our relationship and bond. They'd worry too much if I was in my alone in my room for long periods of time, or if I stayed too long in the shower they would create fuss and have a meltdown. It frustrated me to see them worry so much about me. I could hear footsteps down the hall, someone entering my room as I slept, tiptoeing around to my side of the bed to see if I was breathing and places a soft kiss on my forehead. I'll open my eyes and see mum tiptoeing out of my room. She repeatedly did this so often, I lost count. I felt so guilty for unloading this stress and worry on my family.

Leading up to the transplant, there were a lot of intense feelings. My siblings were freaking out, but it was something we managed to work through together.

The transition was a stressful learning experience for all and something we learnt to navigate together. I was well aware of the effects this had on my family, but they were here to help and provide an endless amount of support. From the initial prognosis to end of the stem cell treatment, my siblings have always been my protectors, counsellors, supporters, advisors and best friends and I am forever grateful for their love, encouragement, their efforts for staying close and connected.

Reconnecting with extended family and friends was much harder than I thought. I wasn't ready to socialise and pretend everything was OKAY when I certainly wasn't. It was tough. I felt my experience with Scleroderma and spending time in hospital had really alienated me from the people I love and cared for the most. I was very selective of who I wanted to interact with. Sometimes I felt so anxious and vulnerable, it seemed easier to retreat from others. I had unconsciously built a wall around myself. I felt the pressure to be positive, talk openly, and share my experience only frustrated me. I was not brave enough to open my heart to others; it was early days and I lived with the fear of having those uncomfortable conversations, exposing my weaknesses. It takes courage which I had lacked but craved.

In reality, I had closed more doors than opened any.

It was easy to withdraw myself from people. I was not in the mood to take calls, respond to messages or just sit and chat. I had changed. I knew my friends and extended family were disappointed but worried at the same time. I am truly sorry for letting you all down, but I hit rock bottom. I was not ready for the spotlight.

The challenges of the recovery process continued...

It seemed way too hard finding my way back to being normal again. The reunion of coming home meant embracing my new life, spending time with family and friends, accepting what happened to me, dealing with the major changes in my life, easing my way back into a routine and rebuilding myself again... but it required hard work and effort.

For the most difficult days, I would lay in bed and rest. I was napping a fair bit. I rarely had an appetite. Taking a shower left me exhausted. It was taking me a while to regain my strength and energy back. The physical effects of my condition triggered a lot of unsettling and depressed feelings, often feeling sad and hopeless.

Like most people after a Stem Cell Transplant, I became very self-conscious of my physical appearance and it was eating away at my self-confidence. I spent a great deal of time worrying about my weight, at the time I only weighed 42 kilos and I continued to struggled to keep food down.

I was eager for a speedy recovery; I hated the way I looked, which added to my self-esteem issues. I remember gazing into bathroom mirror and thought 'I am so ugly'. I wanted to look and feel pretty again. I felt worthless. I was intimidated by the all pretty girls, but then I had to remind myself I am not like other girls. I did not trust my body as it was taking too long to heal itself. With no hair on my head, skin pigmentation under my eyes, on my cheeks, hands and chest, I was distressed about feeling so unattractive. I could barely look at myself in the mirror.

By now you will have realised my journey of self-discovery had been a complete failure.

My human spirit is crushed.

Every time I identified a positive thought, I'd crush it somehow. It was clearly obvious I had a problem with myself. I was a complete mess.

I needed a breakthrough. There was no magic pill to fix what I was going through, I was imploding. I needed to find myself again.

Then the unexpected happened…

I woke up with a fever of 49. I had difficulty breathing, throbbing headache, body aches and pains, cold chills with abdominal pain from the chest cavity to my pelvic area. The pain would come and go, it was very discomforting. I just got out of the bathroom and when I returned to my bedroom, I lost consciousness and passed out. It happened so quickly. My brother witnessed the fall and he screamed out in apparent horror. Mum called the ambulance and within minutes they had arrived to take me to hospital. By the time we reached the hospital, my temperature had dropped to 43. We arrived at the emergency and a team of doctors were waiting for us. It wasn't long before a canella was inserted into my arm and blood was drawn out. During this time, I was sedated with morphine to ease the pain in my abdomen; but it was persistent unremitting pain, I had wrapped my arms around my stomach as I cried and screamed helplessly… as nurses and physicians listened to the sounds of cries as they went about their duties. Meanwhile the senior physician on duty made contact with the Transplant team at St Vincent's Hospital and spoken with my haematologist Dr John Moore. The decision is made to transfer me via ambulance to St Vincent's Hospital.

I felt helpless in my current state, I couldn't hold back the tears. A drug was infused into my canella and within seconds my vision was all blurry, I had no control of my body and I could no longer move. My entire body was all numb. I lost my ability to speak, but my heart was still racing. I squinted my eyes to make sense of what I was seeing ahead of me, but I couldn't make out the people standing in front of me were my family. They were talking to me but I couldn't respond, I could only hear their voices. Soon after, darkness swooped in and I could no longer see the light. I fell asleep as I was wheeled into an Ambulance and taken to St Vincent's Hospital.

I am paralysed in my current state.

I woke to find myself in the hospital ward of St Vincent's hospital with all these familiar faces around me. The nurses working the morning shift were very surprised to see me. I didn't anticipate I would be back in hospital reliving my experience again. Blood cultures were collected, and tests confirmed my white cells had dropped. For the next few days intravenous fluids of antibiotics and hydration were flushed into my immune system. Other tests such as urine and ultrasound were carried out to look for signs of infections. The haematologist recommended CT scan for abdomen; test results confirmed constipation in the abdomen.

It was just one bad experience after another. My prayers to Allah all began with, 'Why is this happening to me again?' I wanted to be home in my own bed. I felt like there was no escape and my body was constantly failing me. How many more bad days, weeks and months will I encounter? At what point does it get better?

I should be on the road to recovery, but I'm far from it.

The recovery process was extremely daunting, triggering stress and anxiety. Hopelessness was consuming me. It was one setback after another. I had set myself up for disappointment. It became harder for me to trust my body. It had betrayed me so many times and was constantly letting me down. It was difficult for me to gain a positive perspective to heal my deepest wounds, and help me find peace, love and gratitude.

I needed some balance here. How was I to make plans for my future, set realistic goals when I am constantly faced with these health challenges? My mind floats into a state of worry and sadness.

My health is not improving, no matter how hard I try.

I had two options, either accept and live with the uncertainties of my life and grow and evolve into a better version of myself, or wallow in my own misery and surrender to Scleroderma.

Ten days later, I left the hospital ward with another bag of medication. This time I was so sure I would not be returning to the hospital.

My relapse had a big impact on my family, but they handed it exceptionally well.... I on the other hand felt immensely guilty and responsible for disrupting their lives. Roles, routines, and responsibilities had suddenly changed. It was a very challenging time for all, they simply had to learn to adjust to these new routines. I feel I have caused them an immense pain of heartache, stress and fear. I really hate that we had to go through this journey together. I just wanted us to live a happy, normal life. It was bad enough I got sick, but this was certainly not fair on them, when they were desperately trying so hard to put on a brave face, but it was significantly impacting their lives in almost every way.

My pain had suddenly become their pain too. Their ongoing support, love and willingness to go the extra mile is what I needed to help push through this life-changing experience. The encouragement and support is what pulled me from the rubble.

Even with all this going on, they helped me to deal with my health issues one step at a time and also I took it upon myself to REALLY see though my commitment of self-improvement, with the view that *it's okay if things don't work out because I don't intend of giving up.*

Suddenly I had become my personal life coach.

As hours turned into days, and days turned into weeks, and weeks turned into months I was slowly figuring out who I was and building on my strengths. My self-discovery journey mattered, I unconditionally accepted this new version of my life and opened my heart to the good and bad that comes from it. In my darkest hours, I was building up my confidence, self-worth and value, replacing negative thoughts with positive thoughts which took a lot of self-practice, slowly reducing my stress and anxiety levels to help improve my mood. I mourned and grieved the loss of my old self, looking back through past photos until I decided it was time to let go of who I once was and I deleted all my photos. To fill the space of loneliness, I let people into my life revealing my vulnerability and openly sharing my story for a deeper healing process. When there were tough times I'd find a way to manage and pick myself up again, learn to adapt to this new version of my life whatever that should be to take the first steps to get my life back on track, see the joy for the littlest things, gain a new perspective of my new life and above all seeing a positive image of myself and finding contentment along the way.

One morning she woke up a different person.

It was important for me to regain my mental and physical health, this meant adopting a strict approach to healthy living.

I took some time each day to focus on improving my mental health and well-being. This also included exercise and physical activities. I was slowly evolving into a better version of myself, discovering what I could and couldn't do and what works for my body.

It was important for me to love and respect by body; I accepted my body had changed, and I respected it with dignity and it was important for me to meet its needs. My self-care journey begins with eating a well balanced diet, with plenty of fruits, vegetables nuts and lentils that are essentially important to help boost my immune system. I'd exercise at a pace that didn't exhaust all my energy and help to increase blood flow so I would feel more energetic. I'd use stretches to help me get through my daily errands. I loved sleeping in, so I would sleep up to 7-8 hours per day and I'd wake up feeling good!

I also surrounded myself with positive people who recognise my worth and shared similar goals, I'd read positive inspirational quotes daily. When my mind naturally wandered to negative thoughts, I'd remind myself what I have been through and replace these thoughts with positive ones and talk to my body, connect with it and understanding what it needs and wants, be kind, show it love and appreciation and set realistic goals and see them through.

Healthy living also involves healthy hygiene. My meals are prepared fresh daily to avoid food poisoning. The house is always kept cleaned. I'll frequently wash my hands also ensure my gums, teeth and mouth are well cared for to avoid mouth ulcers and other oral infections. I'd also take precautions whilst sitting in the sun and limit the amount of time I spend in the sun to avoid getting sun burnt. My skin was highly sensitive after chemotherapy.

For the first three months, I travelled back and forth to the hospital for my fortnightly visits. The follow-up appointments are mandatory to ensure my cell counts have returned to normal. This also includes vital check-ups of blood pressure, temperature, heart rate and weight. The haematologist also reviews my medications, further testing and scans are essential to see how well my internal organs are functioning.

The lead up to the first follow up appointment was quite nerve-wracking. I was worried. I had trouble sleeping, spent so much time tossing and turning. Thinking about the hospital triggered terrible memories, memories that will never leave me. I hated that place!

Both my parents came along. The haematologist was very pleased with my progress. He reduced my medications from twenty pills a day to eight pills daily. I was thrilled with the good news, popping down pills is not so incredibly easy.

As months progressed, my fortnightly visits to the hospital soon became monthly visits. Each time we went back for my regular check-up, my health was gradually improving and I was feeling good about it. The best news I received is when the haematologist gave me the okay to leave the house and that the next follow up appointment would be 12 months later.

My self-discovery journey continued. I was not sure what tomorrow will bring, but it was my responsibility to add some meaning to my life, doing the best I can with what I have. I made some adjustments to my daily routine that will help me find my baseline to happiness again. A care plan that would be helpful for my personal growth. No matter how many times I'd fall, I always get back up again. Turning each setback into an opportunity.

I continued to work through my care plan.

My self-care plan is designed to reduce my symptoms of stress, anxiety and overcome any insecurities and fear I may have associated with the transplant. My inward focus is to feel better about myself again and improve physical, mental and emotional health. I vary the use of these tools depending on how my day plays out, each day is never same.

While I am slowly building up on my energy and physical

strength, I am constantly reminding myself what really matters here, my quality of life, health and happiness. Tough times may seem overbearing, but it's just a process I need to go through to find my way.

Simple steps for self-improvement / self-care: I begin with making a conscious effort —

- Get out of bed before 10am

- Make time for myself, treat myself with love

- Laugh and smile more

- Eat healthy and maintained a well-balanced diet

- Exercising everyday

- Change of scenario: getting out of the house — get some fresh air / go for a walk / visit family and friends

- Listening to my inner voice: Levels of encouragement, positive words. Be honest and true to oneself and stop comparing myself to others. Identifying negative talk and replacing it with positive self-talk

- Set small realistic goals and timeframes to help myself grow and evolve into the person I want to be — focus on my needs and wants

- Make an effort to spend quality time with family and friends. Taking calls, showing an interest, connecting and spreading the love

- Apply makeup and wear clothes that make me feel good

- Watch funny movies, read books, listen to music — dance. Find a new hobby. Step outside my comfort zone

- Do things that make me happy. Doing the things that help to inspire and motivate me to push forward, giving me the added boost I need to get better

  ○ Engaging in all fun and exciting activities to help improve my mental health and well-being

  ○ Join a support group with people who share similar experiences / share experiences with family and friends

  ○ Learn to live the in present

I have always been afraid and uncomfortable with change, so it was only natural for me to have a meltdown, but then I remind myself that nothing lasts forever and this is part of my process to self-recovery.

PART 7: MY NEW IMPROVED DIET/EXERCISE

IN PART ONE I mentioned I have a Lebanese heritage.... well there is no such thing as a Lebanese diet... but our Lebanese foods are made up of whole grains, lamb or goat meat, vegetables, garlic, olive oil, kafta, lemon juice, red meat, chickpeas, eggplant, beans, parsley, falafel, zucchini baba ghanouj, rice, tabouli, fattoush, shawarma, hummus, nuts, just few of many. Cinnamon is added into a variety of foods.

My meals were prepared fresh daily. Mum was eager to fatten me up, but my taste buds were completely off so the food didn't taste so good. Prior to the transplant I had lost a fair bit of weight, during and after chemo I also shredded a few more kilos. Restoring my digestive system back to normal has been one of my biggest challenges. Dietary adjustments were essential, even mum's homemade cooking didn't do the trick. A hospital dietary protein form was recommended. Mum continued to follow the food chart given to us from the hospital of all the foods that I could eat, to ensure body received all the proteins, minerals and vitamins needed to make a full, speedy recovery. I was finally gaining weight, much to my family's relief, including mum who was on a mission to get me married, which I will come back to later on.

One thing I terribly missed was the shisha, commonly known as the hubbly bubbly/hookah or agileh. Before I got sick, I'd smoke the shisha with my father for fifteen minutes a day. It was another thing we had in common. The shisha is well known among men and women. It is socially trending in restaurants, coffee shops, etc. Over the years the shisha has become increasingly popular, especially in my extended family. My relatives including my father have a carry-on bag for their shishas and bring them along to all family gatherings.

What's a party without Shisha?!

Regardless of the event, whether it is a Friday night footy, men sitting around a table playing card game of 400, Sunday afternoon barbeque, Ramadan feast or a birthday party, men and some young women will be smoking the agileh blowing out smoke that lingers in the air for a few seconds. Meanwhile on the other side of the house, kids will be playing games, older women in the kitchen preparing afternoon desserts and Lebanese tea, their conversations will be interrupted with a loud cheer, clapping and shouting coming from the outdoor entertainment area... it seems Parramatta eels had scored a goal or someone had been caught cheating in the card game of 400.

PART 8: SCLERODERMA UPDATE POST-TRANSPLANT

I CONSIDERED MYSELF extremely lucky to be alive. I survived the transplant, and I found improvements with my skin in areas of body. The disease is no longer affecting my joints; I had reduced inflammation in my arms, legs, elbows, kneecaps and wrists. I could get out of bed without support, walk up and down the stairs, dress myself, have a shower, make myself a cup of tea, lift my arms over my shoulders, I could pick myself up from the floor and bend my knees.

The skin of my hands is still very firm and has not softened after the transplant, my fingers are very much curled in, in a claw like shape what is known as Sclerodactyly. They will never be straight again. I cannot make a fist or open them, but that's okay! I am proud and blessed I have made in this far. I still had some minor issues with acid reflux and a CT scan confirmed some lung scarring, but all was manageable and I am free, happy and in control of my life.

I guess you could say that my quality of my life significantly improved following the transplant and I was *FINALLY* in a good place mentally and emotionally. My experiences with Scleroderma were unforeseen and out of my control, but now I had regained a sense of clarity in my life.

Day by day my condition gradually improves. I am getting better. The progression of the disease has ceased. I can proudly say I am no longer bedridden. One thing I have learnt is that we don't realise how good we have it until it's taken away from us. I am profoundly grateful to Allah that I have the ability to walk and feel no pain. It brings me such joy and tears to my eyes. I feel I am almost normal again and blessed that I have been given a second chance at life. Every day I am becoming stronger and I am convinced life from here will only get better.

My illness with Scleroderma has significantly altered my perspective on life. I have come to understand that this illness does not define who I am or how I plan to live my life. This experience has empowered me to live the life the way I want. This exciting new transformation will take me to places where I have never been to before. I am on a mission to embrace this new meaning of life, to become the better version of me, my new and improved self.

I now have a bucket list of things to do, all these exciting things waiting for me. Through hardship, I come to realise the impossible is possible. I am exactly where I need to be right now. Who knows, maybe I am wrong, but for now this is all I've got and I work with it.

Adjusting to new my life also means learning to accept my new energy levels and trusting that they will gradually improve. The healing is a long process, and I had to make some temporary adjustments to my routine when things failed. I definitely had more good days than bad days. I had to deal with a few restrictions. Even though the restrictions were temporary, I had to remind myself it was a minor sacrifice. I had the rest of my life to enjoy the best things of life and stop wasting time whinging and complaining when things didn't work out or go to plan.

I'll continue to allow myself to feel and express my emotions, this was crucial for my path to self-discovery. It was important for me to acknowledge my emotional awareness to avoid strong feelings of anxiety that could lead to a depressive state causing much more serious problems for me.

I even tried mediating and found it really helpful. I would relax my muscles, close my eyes, and focus on breathing exercises, inhaling in and out. It didn't work at first but after a few attempts I found my rhythm and it worked.

I continued to maintain a healthy diet and exercise regularly. I spent most of time at the local indoor pool working out on my legs and arms. Some days I had the pool to myself and after my workout I'll float on my back and close my eyes. I was floating in heated pool and I found the floating experience very calming and peaceful. I also joined my local gym, I spent two to three times a week at the gym doing light cardio exercises.

It's taken me a great deal of time to return to everyday activities. In the beginning it was a challenging, always having to go back to hospital as an outpatient for regular blood work. Constant worrying about relapsing and also trying to figure out the new me. We all cope differently after a transplant, some people return to their normal activities and life goes on, and for some others it can be a long emotional recovery process.

I often wondered if it would be possible for me to bounce back to my normal self again the, 'fun, independent, ambitious, adventurous person', that I was, but I then realised I was far from it. *I had to let go of who I once was.* I pushed myself so hard to outlive the odds, so that I could return to my old life and self, but how wrong was I… my setback did not fit the jigsaw puzzle of my old life.

I had to make room for my new life and fill in the new pieces of the puzzle….

I was learning to survive with the disease and not let it *"OWN ME"*. I am on a mission to be more resilient and adaptable. When people ask me how I am doing, I can now smile and say, *'I am actually doing well, and very pleased with my progress'.*

Although life has not been easy for me, I am happy to report that I no longer feel any pain and I am hopeful it remains this way. I am ready to take on all life experiences, good or bad and accept my new normal and learn how to manage it.

I pray that one day a cure will be found to help others like myself struggling to stay alive from this dreadful disease.

Thank you Allah, for helping me find acceptance

Thank you for easing my pain and suffering

Thank you for restoring my strength, renewing my mind and body

Thank you for surrounding me with the people that love and adore

Thank you for protecting me as one of your children.

PART 9: 100 DAYS - POST STEM CELL TRANSPLANT

I am relieved I have survived my first 100 days.

MY FIRST OUTING was exactly 100 days after my stem cell transplant. I was on my way to the shopping centre to buy some new summer clothes. I was wearing a medical face mask which covered my nose and mouth, and for the first time ever I wore a wig. The shopping centre was busy. It was that time of the year December 2015, Christmas was only a few weeks away.

As soon as I entered the mall, I got all anxious, but I quickly took control of the situation. I had to remind myself to remain calm and to slowly take a deep breathe in and out.

The most common and unpleasant experience of wearing a face mask is catching people staring at you and making uncompassionate remarks. I recall two young male teenagers staring and laughing at me, faking a cough and sneeze as I walked past them. Situations like these are very discouraging and daunting but overall, it felt good to finally leave the house after three months and eat at a nice restaurant with my family.

My reason for wearing a wig is because I could not embrace the bald look. Whenever I left the house I wore my wig. Most of the time I wore my wig to the shopping centre and family gatherings, but when I was home I wore a head cap. It was difficult to wear a wig to the beach especially in summer, my head was always sweating. It was also hard on windy days too; I'd hold on to my wig so it wouldn't blow away. It was impossible to go swimming in a wig. Through my experiences, I've learnt the painful realities of wearing a wig. But I was not ready to give up the wig just yet. I tried really hard to acknowledge the girl in the mirror with no hair, but it was harder than I thought. I felt less attractive, and the baldness was merely unavoidable.

My levels of energy varied from day to day. Some days I had massive amounts of energy. My cousins would come over with their nerf guns, and surprisingly I would find myself chasing them in the front yard of the house and firing bullets back, being silly. It was fun and I enjoyed it.

It's been a long time since I felt this way.

As weeks turned into months, my condition continued to improve and I came to realise having my health back, being alive and surviving the transplant outweighs the baldness. I finally got used to embracing the 'bald look'. I could finally look at my reflection in the mirror with total acceptance.

One summer morning I woke up, I made eye contact with my reflection in the mirror and I saw a pretty bald girl with a full set of eyebrows looking back at me. I saw a vision of beauty, my own kind of beauty... But this pretty girl had sad eyes, and a story waiting to be told.

Funny enough, I never lost my eyebrows during my chemotherapy sessions. I was very fortunate. It took almost a year for me to acknowledge how attractive I am as bald chick. Wig or no wig, I realised *'I am beautiful'* and no one can convince me otherwise.

I accept myself as I am, I have made peace with my past, I am learning to love myself more and more each day. I am enough, I love my flaws and imperfections, I am worthy of love, I am beautiful with my imperfect body, this is me and I am constantly growing and evolving into a better version of myself.

At that moment, I removed my self-care practise post-it note from my mirror and scrunched it up...

I was growing impatient with my daily routine; I was eager to return to work and move forward with my new life, but I still had to face the physical challenges that came with my disease such as the digital ulcers on my fingers, constant fatigue, my energy levels, stress and cold environments triggering a Raynauds attack. I was also cautious of public places with large crowds and had to avoid eating out to protect myself from food poisoning.

My next follow up appointment with the haematologist was scheduled for mid-January 2016. The specialist was very pleased with my progress. He was so impressed with my blood work that he reduced medications to only one tablet and approved for me to return to work, part-time only. Surprised by the doctor's comments, I sprang from my seat with excitement, which made the doctor laugh.

I was finally going back to work, a place of familiarity to a job I really enjoyed. This was the distraction I needed, but then suddenly the thought of going back to work became unsettling, I felt sick in the stomach.

PART 10: GOING BACK TO WORK

————————

I've turned the corner, and I am not looking back. I am driven by my plan to get my life back on track. Staying focus right now is all that matters. I am ready for my return to the office.

I GOT THIS…

THE DECISION TO go back to work was within my control, it was a positive choice for me, and support was available to easy my way in. I was so sure I was ready to take this leap. It was important for me to build my confidence and increase my motivation during this transition. I was excited to be going back and embrace the commute... yep I really didn't mind it. Going back to work was another big achievement. I was very diligent and persistent to attain these important goals in my life.

In February 2016, I returned to the Sydney CBD office. I was dressed for success. I had planned my outfit the night before and picked out a nice pair heels. I looked good and I felt great. The commute to the city was a two hour journey from my house. I was listening to music that I downloaded onto my iPhone. I looked outside the window thinking about my last train ride into the city prior to the transplant and how much pain I had been in. As the train pulled into the station, I slowly made my way to the exit holding onto the railing with a memory of a flashback that comes and goes. I was surrounded by so many commuters getting in and out of the train, making their way to their offices. As I reached the escalator there was a long trail of commuters waiting to get on and I joined the queue but I am faced with one flashback after another as I make my way to the office.

Ten minutes later, I am standing inside the foyer of my old building. It seems as though nothing has changed, but everything about me has. I returned my access card prior to my exit back in 2015, so on my arrival I called my manager to let him know I have arrived and I was waiting for him in the foyer.

As we made our way to the escalators heading to level twenty-eight, I am greeted by onlookers that looked oddly familiar but I could not recall their names. When we reached our floor, I am greeted by a group of colleagues I've known for years with hugs and kisses. On my way to my desk, I notice very little had changed in the office, just some new faces and some minor changes to the office layout, but everything else remained the same.

Returning to work after taking sick leave was good for my mental health. I was still digging bald chick look but I could not overlook the social shyness of being bald and having all eyes on me. I'd remind myself it's just all in my head but I felt awkward walking around the office with my bald look so I made the decision to wear a wig on my first day back.

My return to work was not straightforward. I knew I had to make temporary changes to the number of hours and days I worked. It was important for me to do things right at my own pace, and also follow the doctor's orders.

The morning of my arrival, I was sitting in my line manager's office and we discussed my 'return to work' plan. I raised my concerns with my employer and he was happy for me to return to three days a week, with the intention of picking up a fourth day in the coming months, only if my doctor approved it. My employer also agreed to flexible working conditions, so I could make appointments in between work hours if needed.

My transition back to work was far from perfect. The biggest struggle was in my inability to concentrate on my work and the constant fatigue. It seemed so exhausting. Some days were emotionally challenging too. I was doubting myself if I could do the job and deliver results. I realised I had made the mistake of going back to work too soon. I set unrealistic goals and expectations for myself, going back to work required a lot of energy and effort. I felt that I rushed this process, when my energy should only have been focussed on ME, improving my health and physical state, instead of trying to manage a mini project. At work I felt compelled to be perfect, but I was far from it.

I feel very sluggish in work duties.

It took me some time to adjust into new work life, and find a routine that was manageable and gradually settle in. As days turned into weeks, I found myself adapting quickly to the work life balance, making some adjustments to the way I work, monitoring my mental health and work progress at the same time. My health mattered, it was my responsibility to look after myself and continue working towards my journey of self-discovery. I was slowly discovering my true strengths and my limits.

Once I had settled in, I received very little support from employer and it soon became impossible to work with him. My return to work plan fell through the cracks...

He set up a meeting to discuss my performance but noted it was an informal catch-up. In the meeting he raised his concerns that we had a number of projects in the pipeline and wanted me to commit to four days a week, which I was certainly not prepared for. I suggested he hire more staff and he advised that recruitment was in progress and our new starters would commence at the end of the month. I expressed to my employer that I was not in position to pick up another day's work. It was not in my best practise to take on this kind pressure and it seemed unfair. I attempted to reason with him, but he made it perfectly clear that if I refused to pick up the additional shift, he would terminate my contract. I had 2 weeks to make a decision.

There is no sympathy or humanity from this guy.

As the days went on, my workload increased and I was overwhelmed by the number of tasks given to me by my employer. I found myself working to exhaustion, skipping breaks and forgetting to drink water. In our previous discussion, I reminded him what I had been through to be here today and that I would appreciate some support and compassion but he responded with, *'but you look fine to me'*. I realised if I had accepted to work four days a week, it was only a matter of time before he insist I work 5 days a week. I felt singled out because of my health condition. It was total discrimination, this was harassment and bullying. His behaviour was completely unacceptable and unlawful, and very discouraging.

I mean, it's not like I had a nose job or some Botox around my face.

I lost my motivation for work and I felt as though I was dragging myself into the office. Some nights I was tossing and turning I couldn't fall asleep, thinking about work and the stressors of the day that were yet to come. In that short period, I was physically and mentally drained to the point where I had to put an end to this. I was mindful of what I needed to do in this difficult situation. I could no longer tolerate his negativity and uncompassionate ways.

I requested a meeting with my employer and submitted my resignation.

The transition of returning back to work had not been a smooth and easy process, especially when I was trying so hard to adapt to my new life that Allah has rewarded me with.

June 30th 2016 would be my final day in the office. I was very disappointed because I was leaving a job that I actually enjoyed and the benefits of work played a crucial role in my sense of identity and purpose. It was the distraction I need from Scleroderma. When I am at work, I am not thinking about my health or what it feels like to be fighting with your own body. I forget the pain, my time spent in hospital, and I'm not sitting in the dark corner of my bedroom while my mind plays tricks on me. I forget what it feels like to watch life go on as I wallow in my misery or my inner thoughts and anxiety.

Despite my employer's behaviour, I worked in a safe environment with some amazing people that were very supportive; I felt accepted. I had become one of them; I felt valued and appreciated by others.

Leading up to my departure, I ran into a senior leader from my organisation (I'll call him Mr X) that I had previously worked with. I found myself sitting in his office sharing my health experience with him and discussing my work situation. He was really disappointed by how the situation was handled and took it upon himself to follow up with my employer, not that I was expecting him too. He just wanted to help. A few days later my contract was extended with the agreement I could work up to three days a week, depending on how I was feeling. I would also have the flexibility to work one day from home, and I could leave the office during work hours for doctor's appointments. As such, I would no longer have to report to my old line manager because Mr X was now my new reporting manager.

I was very grateful for this opportunity and pleased with the amount of support I had received from Mr X, and I thanked him repeatedly. He is a great role-model and vision for all leaders; he is kind, inspiring and very compassionate man with a big heart. Thank you for treating me fairly and equally.

From this day forward, I was happy to return to the work environment with a great work/life in balance that would help to boost my morale, improve my physical and mental health. My energy levels were good. Not only did it improve my level of productivity, I was no longer stressed and it was easier for me to sleep again.

To break up the day, I would take short breaks. I'd step outside for some fresh air. I also made an effort to interact and openly share my health journey and challenges with my trusted employees. There was no awkwardness because I was comfortable with the team. They accepted and understood my struggle with this disease and the recovery process of the transplant. Not too long after I was back to my happy, cheerful self.

I finally feel confident and in control of my work environment.

PART 11: HAPPY 1ST RE- BIRTHDAY

*I am healthy and strong. My hair has slowly grown back now.
I weigh 56 kilos. Scleroderma remains steady, I am a survivor.*

*I am so blessed to be alive and breathing. Birthdays have
always been significantly important to me and my family. It's
a memorable moment; I love the cakes, parties and presents.
After my life-changing experience with Scleroderma and Stem
Cell Transplant, birthdays now symbolize much more to me.*

*I fight this battle every day to celebrate
my birthday with my loved ones.*

So Happy 1st Re-Birthday to me.

SEPTEMBER 30TH 2016 marked one year since my Stem Cell Transplant.

I learnt to embrace my new birthday as it reminds me of what I have been through, and appreciate the fact I am still alive. *I am happy and doing well.* Good things have happened. My hair is finally growing back and I am no longer wearing a wig. Work is great, but Most importantly my battle with Scleroderma remains stable. Some days have been harder than others. Everyday thoughts popped into my head about my future and my loved ones, and I found myself hoping I'll still around for important milestones. I've been over-whelmed with the amount of love and support I have received from family and friends. I am blessed and grateful to have my family. I survived another year to appreciate their hugs, kisses, laughter and unconditional love. Despite what I had been through, I was making a big effort to be comfortable with the uncertainty, accepting that I don't know what the future will bring, but loving where I am right now in my life. Spending quality time with my family and friends, as if it was my final days on earth.

Scleroderma update - I am fortunate enough to have responded well to treatment, hospital follow-ups are now yearly visits. Although the worst part is finally over, I still have some bone pain and some stiffness in my wrist. The rheumatologist has put me back on to prednisone 10mg alternating days to help ease inflammation and swelling. I am still maintaining a healthy balanced lifestyle; I am lot calmer, motivated and stronger than ever. Then the most extraordinary thing happened to me... one morning I woke up to find blood in between my legs. I finally got back my periods back.

I was so overwhelmed with joy. I thought perhaps this may be too much to share in my book, but it is, after all, a big part of my journey, and to understand my story I need to include all events good or bad. I had been waiting a very long time for this day to come. I was certainly not expecting for my period to return. I felt whole, fertile and feminine again, then the cramping started and I was relieved because I was reminded of my old body/self, not that I am complaining. It was a nice feeling; I realised good things were happening to my body, it was finally healing itself.

But my body was nowhere near perfect some days were harder than others, but having so many people pushing for me to get through this life-changing experience, I could not let them down or myself. When I was at my lowest and weakest point, I turned to my faith. It was the one thing I could truly count on.

I've learnt powerful and the greatest lessons though life experiences. I have dealt with some tough situations and believe this is Allah's way of testing my faith through hardship, to see how much I could truly handle. So I prayed religiously day and night, and read chapters from the Holy Quran. As each day passed, I learnt how to shift my mindset to embrace change, to go from an unhappy person to becoming a more positive individual, wanting more and striving to be better person. To transform the way I see things and how I wish to live my life. I came to understand the purpose of my life. The Holy Quran's teaching has helped me to find meaning in my life, to be patient for the unexplained events and suffering. Through Allah's guidance, I am learning to open my heart and find myself again, to love and value my body. Today I feel much closer to my faith. Allah has given me the patience and strength to deal with the negativity of this disease. I finally feel in control. My faith has helped me to adapt and find acceptance with the disease.

My fears have helped me to find a deep appreciation for life, even from unpleasant events. Being a positive person, I am determined to see the good even during the bad times.

PART 12: YEAR 2017 – MY JOURNEY WITH SCLERODERMA CONTINUES...

I am fine one day and sick the next. I am somewhat positive, but there are days I feel defeated; I am afraid of relapsing. The road has not been easy. My battle with Scleroderma continues, and I have learnt to accept it. I understand I am no longer a healthy person.

When I look in a mirror, I am reminded of the struggles I have been through just to stay alive.

MY BODY FUNCTIONALITY had changed and my appearance too. My condition with Scleroderma is affecting the skin in other areas of my body and causing joint pain. At this moment, I have become very self-conscious about my appearance again. I felt my confidence was declining in stages and my self-esteem was under attack.

Scleroderma is back to steal my beauty, identity and my life

A chest scan of the lungs confirmed some severe scarring. By late 2017, I was diagnosed with Interstitial Lung Disease (ILD). Interstitial lung disease is irreversible and is associated with a chronic cough and shortness of breath, either when resting or engage in some type of activity. I sat in my family doctor's office as he conveyed the news to me from the medical report. As I blankly stared at him lost for words, tears flooded my eyes and he offered me tissue, assuring me it was going to be okay. All I could do was nod my head in acceptance, but I knew this was the beginning of my so called self-discovery journey to unhappy life.

I walked out of his surgery and headed to the parking a lot. My hands were trembling as I tried to unlock the car door, but instead the keys fell through my hands and hit the concrete floor. Once I was in my car, I burst into tears. I probably cried for a good solid ten to fifteen minutes before I turned on the ignition, put the brake into drive and headed home, unsure of how I would convey this bad news to my family.

I am torn and I don't know what to make of it.

I finally arrived home, I opened the door and walked in with a smile on my face. I was excited to see my nieces and nephew standing by window on the floor, looking out through the blinds calling out to me, 'Aunty Coco is home'. Their presence is a fullness of joy. My adorable nieces with curls are both under five years, wore matching outfits with stains of chocolate ice cream melted on their dresses and chocolate smeared across their faces. Meanwhile, my sister-in-law is chasing the youngest around the house to wash her chocolatey hands and face. The oldest giggled at the sight of her mother chasing her sister around the kitchen table and walked away with a bowl of chips and marshmallows handed down to her from one her uncles. Their eating habits is something my five-year-old nephew can't seem to grasp as he leans over and whispers into my ear, 'why do they always eat so much?' with the ps3 hand controller in his right hand and raspberry Zooper Dooper wrapped with in white serviette paper in his left hand. Meanwhile, his charming smile, good looks and smart mouth gets him out of trouble. He is so beautiful he makes my heart melt.

I escape the loud chatter, giggling children pacing around the house and make my way to my bedroom, which is at the end of the hallway. I walk into my room and settle at the edge of my bed, staring blankly at the wall for a few seconds before I close my eyes and wished my life took a different turn. But I had to face the reality, this was another setback and yes... the most devastating news ever but something I had to endure now for the rest of my life.

Why is this continuing to happen to me? How and why did I relapse so quickly?

My heart is aching.

I gently broke the news to my family. I felt so guilty overwhelming them with such bad news. Mum cried helplessly, and I also learnt that a few days prior to the transplant, my father cried helplessly to my mother and sister. I feel utterly responsible for their sadness and grief. They have encountered so much in a short period of time.

My scleroderma makes me feel I am a burden to my family, and it hurts. I am frustrated for my family. They are stuck with my misery; it drains me and I know it's destroying them.

To ease the chronic cough and shortness of breath, my family doctor prescribes salbutamol inhaler up to four times a day and Fluticasone/salmeterol daily.

One day I was working in one of the metro offices, and the practise fire drill bell rang. The chief wardens of the floor urges the employees to use the stairs and I let out a deep sigh of disappointment.

It was a walk down memory lane...

We headed to the large staircase on the twelfth floor and slowly made our way to the ground floor as I held on the railing. By the time we had reached the basement and made our way to the front entrance of the building, my heart was pounding and I experienced shortness of breath. Thirty minutes passed before we were instructed to head back into the building and I was relieved we could use the lifts.

The stairs is just one of many examples where I found myself out of breath gasping for air, feeling exhausted as though I had been running for miles. This often happens with walking long and short distances too.

PART 13: YEARS 2018 / 2019

NOTHING IS EVER simple with Scleroderma. As the year progressed so did my symptoms of scleroderma. Some days my voice was
croaky, I continuously had to clear my throat. Stress and cold temperatures triggered Raynauds attacks. If you live with chronic pain,
you'll understand what it feels like to wake up each day with symptoms of body aches, pains and stiffness. I have a number of digital
ulcers on my fingers that were breaking out. I had bumped them a
few times and they were painfully sore. I still encountered some minor
acid reflux issues.

I have been on prednisone since 2016 to alleviate pain. It took
me some time to get off prednisone, but I immediately ceased it after
discovering I had osteoporosis. I am young but feel decades older.
I felt trapped in the body of a 70-year-old woman, it's a terrifying
experience threatening my independence but I had to maintain a
hopeful and positive outlook instead of worrying about what was yet
to come. I had already accomplished so great things; I was adamant
to continue down this rough and bumpy road.

It's so ironic how I love winter, but I suffer the most from the
cold. Yes, as crazy as it sounds considering my health situation and
my sensitivity to the cold. Cozying up in front of the heater, eating
a bowl of ice cream and wearing tons of layers, while it's raining
outside is what I absolutely love doing. In my household, I am the
person who hogs the heater, the warm air blowing in my face is
like heaven.

One winter morning I woke up at 5am to the sounds of the wind
whistling through the trees. A cold front had blown through the
night and it was freezing cold. I didn't want to get out of bed; I was
so warm, I rugged up in thick fur bedcovers all fleecy and soft. I had
no energy or motivation to get out of bed, but then I remembered
I had tons of work to get through for the day. I crawled out of bed,
making my way to the bathroom to get ready for work. An hour and
a half later I was headed to the kitchen to prepare my breakfast when

my knees gave away and I had a sudden fall. Thankfully, I didn't break any bones. I still managed to get into the office, I had to keep moving forward despite the mild pain in my leg. The following week I made an appointment to see an endocrinologist and he prescribed a drug injection called Prolia to help reduce the risk of fractures and to increase bone mass density. Prolia should not be used if you are pregnant or planning to get pregnant. It will potentially harm the baby and lead to serious complications with the pregnancy, or worse, lead to a miscarriage. I made the decision not to proceed with the treatment. I still had some hope of becoming a mother. A girl can dream right? Once Prolia is injected into the bloodstream, it will take several years for it to wear off, potentially impacting my chances of falling pregnant.

I continued working up until late September 2019 until I got sick with bronchitis. The flu season was here to stay. Everyone seemed to be getting sick. I had the worse flu symptoms; body aches and pain, fatigue, running nose, dry cough, fever, cold chills and headache. My immune system was terribly weak, and I was feeling miserable. One morning I woke up with a fever of 44. Mum was panicking but she managed to call the ambulance. Ten minutes later two smoking hot paramedics stood in my bedroom and my first thought was, *Omg I am not wearing any makeup, I haven't even brushed my teeth yet.* I caught a glimpse of myself in the mirror and my hair was a total mess. One of the paramedics glanced over to my dressing table. My second thought was, *oh no please don't look there.* It was a mess. My makeup, hairspray, jewellery, facial products and my bra were sitting on top of one another. I was so embarrassed with myself and I noticed his smile was titled to one side and it looked like he was smirking. I put my head down in shame…

I was taken to Wollongong hospital. The nurse drew out some blood from the cannula in my arm and a doctor took a swab sample from the back of my nose, and thirty minutes later I was moved into isolation. I was diagnosed with influenza A and I was told I would remain in isolation until the infection had cleared. It was disappointing to be back in hospital and living in-between the four walls again. Not something I anticipated. Strangely enough, I was calm and in control. Despite what I was going through, I was learning to deal with my daily stresses and the discomforts, and recognised this was part of my process of self-discovery.

I took two weeks off work to recover. This was just another setback to deal with. It wouldn't be long and I would be outside these hospital walls living my life and making new memories again. My ordeal has not been great, but I am constantly reminding myself how far I have come and how the good days always outweigh the bad days, therefore I will manage. Tough times don't last forever, and I had faith in my journey.

It was my responsibility to keep a hold on my peace and sanity in my current state.

I am fearless, while I am still breathing,

My experiences with Scleroderma have made me a more resilient, and determined individual. I feel that I have the strength to face any health issues that come my way. I have learnt to adapt to my new normal ways of living and manage my own pain, I've learnt my limits and how to pace myself. I have set boundaries for my energy levels.

I am very mindful that my life may be cut short at some point in time. *That's absolutely okay.* I accept this and I will not dwell on it. Allah decides when it is my time and for now I will keep on living my life doing what I love best with no regrets.

Up until now, I have lived an eventful life. Many things have happened. I graduated from university. I bought a house and my dream car. I travelled to a few places. I watched my nieces and nephew come into this world and grow up into beautiful souls, and still growing and I am writing my very first book. My one and only deal breaker is not getting married in my late twenties and starting a family of my own.

Whilst I have always remained respectful to my Lebanese Muslim heritage, I also embraced the Australian culture and my parents found ways to compromise too, trying their best to balance out the two cultures and preserve our traditions. My entire childhood was filled with experiences of my cultural customs and social traditions. My siblings and I learnt to speak Arabic at a fairly young age and mum also encouraged us to attend Arabic school, which was held every Saturday morning. We learnt to eat the traditional Lebanese dishes at a young early age, with loath of Lebanese bread with every meal.

We also learnt about the significance of Ramadan and participated in fasting up until midday, and as we got older we'd fast for the whole day and breaking our fast at sunset. We learnt to recite prayers from the holy Quran and celebrate EID, we'd learn the traditional Lebanese dance and dabke. Waking up to the sound of Fairuz singing through the early hours of the morning was common in a Lebanese household, with the rich smell of Lebanese coffee filling the house as it boiled on the stove.

Social habits are if you see a shoe or sandal on its back (wherever you are), you must flip it over, simply because it is improper for the bottom part of the shoe or sandal to be facing up and disrespectful to Allah. Today if I see the bottom part of the shoe/sandal facing up I'll flip it over wherever I am, and if I don't, I'll feel so guilty and ashamed of myself.

Or if you step over a kid's legs, while they are laying on the ground, you'll have to step back over them and reverse it... there is a saying that if you step over a child's leg they will never grow up. Here is another one, if a person is talking about someone (a typical gossip session) and you sneeze, we have a saying that the information about this someone is actually true... simply because of the sneeze.

How about the Lebanese beads (mishbaha) hanging in the car for good luck and protection?

I also learnt the meaning of the word habibi *my love* commonly used in every conversation... it seems everyone is a habibi and I discovered that the word Inshallah *with God's will* can mean different things. For example, 'Mum can I go to the movies with a friend?' and she will respond with, *'Inshallah'* or, 'I am going shopping tomorrow,' they will respond with *'Inshallah'*.

Growing up with traditional Lebanese parents, I did miss out on school discos and sleepovers, but they always made up for it in other ways, allowing me to attend the school camp and invite my friends over. As I grew older, I could attend the school danced being chaperoned by brother. It was a cultural thing, and I just accepted it as it is and went along with it. We had privileges but within their boundaries (I did break a few) and we always complied (majority of the time) with my parent's decisions, though sometimes I would question their decision to understand their reasons behind it.

This one time I was invited to a birthday party from one of the girls in school and I really wanted to go... but I was not too sure if my parents would let me. I entered the living room with the invitation card tucked away in the pockets of my pjs and walked towards the couch sitting directly opposite my parents. Mum had been sewing the hem of my brother's school pants. She looked up and asked if I was okay. They'd been watching a Syrian classic comedy film *Ghawar and Fatoum* and they were drinking (Kahwa) I had rehearsed my plea to attend my friend's birthday party prior to entering the living, but in my head I already knew their answer was no. When I raised the questioned and took out the invitation card from my pocket to show my mum, dad shut it down immediately (arguing that he didn't know the girl's parents) whereas mum had assured dad that it was ok, I would be accompanied by my sister, she would drop us off and meet my friend's mother.

It was important for siblings and I to get an education and mum went to all efforts to hire a private tutor that would earn $20 bucks an hour, eat dinner with us and leave the house with a full bag of leftovers.

My dream to get into university is theirs as well as mine

When I got into university, I made my parents so proud and they felt their hard work had really paid off. For me, the pressure to get married only started in my final year of university. I was in my early twenties and I was certainly not ready for marriage. I had many suitors come forward from Australia and back home in Lebanon, at the time neither of them seemed to be a good match for me or meet my criteria of 'the ideal man'… causing much heartache to my mother who was eager to see me marry after graduating from university and conceive a kid or two. By the time I found my ideal man and was well ready for marriage, Scleroderma struck and changed my life.

I never thought that one morning I would wake up sick and be stuck like this forever.

Before Scleroderma, I always thought of myself as a good-looking person, but it wasn't until when I started university that I actually got noticed. When I was eleven years old, I was teased that I was ugly (I had a one eyebrow, afro hair and a big nose) while my parents would constantly be reminding me that I am beautiful and that person was just being very silly and immature, to simply ignore them. All through secondary school, I truly believed I was ugly and accepted this perception from others too. It explained why I was so shy, insecure and had low self-esteem all through high school. I was incapable of being myself around others, always worried about being judged or criticized for something I said or did.

As a Lebanese Australian girl, I had bushy eyebrows that stood out and covered my face as opposed to my some of peers in high school with naturally shaped pretty eyebrows. Not to mention the abundance of hair on my arms and legs. My legs were so hairy up until ninth grade. Mum refused to let me shave my legs, I'd plead and she would say always no. I was so self-conscious about my hairy legs during P.E and on the days I wore a skirt to school, I was afraid of getting caught out by my high school crush.

The first time I noticed my high school crush, I was standing on the school bridge that connected the maths department to the geography section. I had just stepped out of my one hour maths session with Mr Bush. I hated algebra and trigonometry and I wasn't particularly fond of these topics. My friends and I were headed to the English department crossing the bridge when I noticed a tall boy with board shoulders bouncing a basketball in his hand as he wore his hat back-to-front. I leaned over to one of the girls standing beside me and whispered, 'who is that guy with the basketball in his hand?' She shrugged her shoulders implying that she didn't know, but Jessica overheard our conversation and blurted out 'oh that's XX from my English classes,' as we hurried along to our geography lesson. His name lingers in the back of my head.

My high school crush story was no block buster romantic comedy, XX was handsome and the top of his class in all subjects. He was very talented, popular and always surrounded by the prettiest and snobbiest girls from my year. But we shared one thing in common, our Lebanese heritage. He didn't know I existed, I could have been standing right next to him and he wouldn't notice me. I was not popular, just an ordinary girl with thick curly hair. He and I lived in two different worlds, I would admire him for distance. Sometimes I would see him in the canteen area waiting to be served, I was way too shy to acknowledge him and engage in a conversation..

I never thought a guy like that would notice a girl like me, but he did...

Up until end of year nine, I had hairy legs. I was so embarrassed around my peers I would lay my jumper over my legs hoping no one would notice them. One afternoon I got home from school, I told my mother if she didn't wax my legs, I would take one of dad's razors and shave my legs myself. I was fed up and I couldn't wait anymore longer. I had peers that rolled up their skirts above their knees, showing off their legs and thighs. I'll never forget the night mum waxed my legs…It was Friday night and mum just had heated the wax in the microwave. We waited a few minutes for it to cool down, before slathering the wax on my skin and shortly ripped the hair out by the roots. I screamed a loud tearful cry of agony and with my lips pursed together I started blowing air out of my mouth on to my leg to ease the pain. To be honest, I had anticipated this much pain, but it was all worth it. My legs were so soft and smooth. The following Monday I wore a skirt to school showing off my less so hairy legs hoping my high school crush would notice.

Before the end of the school year I did what any reasonable teenager would do, I refined my eyebrows, learnt how to use the iron to straighten my hair, learnt how to shave my legs without having to ask mum to wax them for me and learnt how to apply light natural makeup ready for the summer holidays. I was embracing this new change and my need to connect to my idea of what is beautiful. I was still the girl with dark brown curly hair, but I had refined features.

I had a nickname for my school crush. My friends and I often referred to him as Curly Wurly, like the chocolate bar for his natural curls. Whenever he walked into a room, my friends would nudge me and whisper, 'Curly Wurly is here'.

One morning, I ran into him on my way to roll call. I was running five minutes late and so was he. We were both headed in the same direction. I was one level above his and we were both running towards stairs, which is directly opposite the canteen. He acknowledges me with a smile and says, 'hello'. I had this jittery feeling in my stomach, my heart was racing... the thought of seeing him from afar did not compare to seeing him up close. I couldn't wait to share this information with my friends. I stuttered the word hello which sounded a lot like, 'cullo', or something of the sort because he laughed. He took quickly off, taking two steps at a time as I also picked up my pace and ran to my roll call class... As the year progressed on, it became a habit of running into each other on the way to roll call. As you all know, small talk can be somewhat challenging, especially when you have a massive crush on someone and you are always worried about what to say next. Our conversations were short, something like, 'Hi so are you Lebanese?' and he would respond with, 'Yeah I am.' In a deep, husky voice he would say, 'my dad is good friends with your uncle'. Other conversations would begin with, 'Are you going to the under eighteens party this week?' just random conversations like this.

In my second final year of high school, we were given the option to select our electives for the year. I was on my way to my first elective, headed towards my business studies class when I walked into the classroom, I was surprised to see Curly Wurly sitting in the back row of the classroom with the popular kids in my year...

I was excited and yet the tiniest bit nervous to see him in the same room. I couldn't hide my emotions, I smiled and I think he saw it...

Why do your friends have to embarrass you front of your crush? They would call out the code name, this makes me cringe, *as if he needs to know his name is Curly Wurly right?* Or how about when he walks pass you and they give you that *Look* making it soo obvious. Or when they keep tabs on him and tell you at lunch, '*We saw Curly Wurly talking to that red-head from legal studies.*' There were times I'd catch him looking my direction, keeping that steady gaze. The gaze made me feel so nervous but I was loving every moment of it. There was an unexplained chemistry between us. As we approached our year 12 formal, Jessica heard a rumour that he would invite me to the formal as his date for our school formal.

I was so excited I was jumping for joy. I could not contain my excitement. The school formal was only six sleeps away, and I was impatiently waiting for him to come and ask me to the formal. The day finally arrived, it was during lunch that he made his way to the front of the school; he was approached by this girl who sat in my group. She questioned why he was standing on our lawn, *as if we owned the school or something…* The conversation only lasted for fifteen seconds, before she ushered him away. I dropped my lunch and quickly ran over to them. He took one glanced at me, I could see that he was angry and annoyed. He stomped away. I called out to him, but he just ignored me. *What happened, what did she say to him?*

She admittedly knew that he was coming to ask me out to the formal but made a joke of the side of his head that really upset me. *He was perfect for me, and I really didn't care what she thought.*

I didn't see him on the night of the school formal, but my sources informed he was there and he arrived alone. I heard a rumour that he hooked up with the red-haired from legal studies a few days before our final yearly exams. The last time I saw Curly Wurly that year was when we were all seated in the school hall for the HSC and we locked eyes for a good five seconds before the bell rang and exam commenced. Three hours later I looked up and was gone.

Would my life have taken a different turn if we had gone to the formal together?

I was in need of a new makeover, so by the time I started university I had coloured my hair, improved the way I applied my makeup and updated my wardrobe... From then on, I could not leave the house without makeup on and my high heels. I was pleased with my new look, and I felt really good about myself. Admittedly, the clothes and makeup helped to boost my confidence, but it also improved my appearance. *It made me realise how attractive I was.* I was attracting attention and every time I opened my mouth people wanted to listen, to hear what I had to say, where my opinion and thoughts mattered. Suddenly feeling beautiful made me more powerful.

One summer afternoon, I was sitting outside the uni bar with a group of friends having lunch waiting for our next class when a tall man with broad shoulders, wearing a hat and backpack on his shoulder walked past the uni bar, headed towards the library. He was looking directly at me. *It was Curly Wurly...* it'd been so long since I last saw him; I had this nervous feeling in the pit of my stomach, suddenly I felt I was back in high school, not knowing if this would be the last time I ever see him again.

Year 2019

Scleroderma continues to affect me in countless of ways...

In April 2019, I returned for my follow-up appointment with the lung specialist. He found 5mm benign nodule in left lung. The specialist recommended an immune suppressant drug called Mycophenolate. Mycophenolate is used to help prevent the rejection of transplant and reduce the progression of autoimmune diseases. I was not ready to commence with the treatment as there are a number of potential side effects with the drug, for examples my blood cells will drop and Mycophenolate may inherently impact my IVF plans.

I was unsure of the doctor's suggested medical advice; I made a decision to seek a second opinion from a lung specialist at St Vincent's Hospital. After reviewing my CT chest scan she suggested trialling 500mg of Mycophenolate daily, which I willingly declined.

On average, I have more good days than bad days. Over the last few months, the back of my knees had become very stiff and sore, causing some issues with my mobility. Thanks to mum, I started using an anti-inflammatory supplement called tumeric which helps to treat a variety of health conditions and is proven to be effective and fast acting. Surprisingly, I found my creaky joints no longer creaked and the pain behind my knees is no longer there.

Eliminating the chronic fatigue is a constant challenge. I started exercising again, but it was a slow process. I'll try to exercise two to three times a week whenever I can. Some days are much harder than others, but I work at a pace that is tailored to my needs and I refused to give up. I respected my body too much and know what it deserves. I lost some weight not by choice, so food absorption continued to be an ongoing issue for me.

Cold weather and stressful events continues to trigger Raynaud's attack restricting blood flow to the fingers causing much discomfort and calcium deposits had grown on my kneecaps, shoulders and wrists which are beyond my control and painfully sore. I started using tea tree oil on my ulcers, which helped to ease pain and dry the open wounds.

I was, and still am faced with the challenges of my claw-like fingers. For instance, I don't have the strength in my fingers to hold a full jug of water or a kettle, I can only carry half full jug of water... The simplest tasks such as opening a bottle of water or jar, opening kitchen cupboards with no handles, cutting up fruit, buttoning up a shirt, putting on a pair of jeans takes ten minutes or so, picking up coins from the floor if I've accidentally dropped them have become quite challenging. But on the plus side, I am still capable of doing many others things such as driving, applying makeup, cooking with some assistance, folding clothes, cleaning, typing on a keyboard, carrying shopping bags, holding a baby, changing a diaper just to name a few.

I know some things cannot be changed such as my stiff claw-like fingers. It is something I have to live with for the rest of my life.

Meanwhile particles of food are entering my lungs from my oesophagus, triggering coughing and vomiting attacks. A visit to rheumatologist has suggested sleeping upright, avoid eating big meals after 6pm and has also increased my Esomeprazole to double the strength.

The facial skin around my mouth is very tight and my mouth had shrunk (Microstomia). I struggle to open my mouth as wide as possible, it also makes it hard trying to chew my food, brush my teeth and dental work. I manage these symptoms with facial exercises.

I am still actively working and commuting via train. Going back to work has helped to improve my mental health. My workplace continues to encourage flexible working. In the last few years I've been working two days from home and three days in the office. I am loving the work/life balance arrangement.

My relationships with certain people have been difficult to maintain. From the onset of my illness, I have learnt who I can truly trust and count on for support, those that understood the illness, and the limitations that come with the disease. There are some people in my life that don't seem to understand what I have been through just to stay alive or how the disease affects my everyday living. It is impossible for me to commit to plans when I am fine one day and sick the next, which is one of the most difficult parts of living with Scleroderma. I know I have disappointed so many people cancelling invitations at the last minute, but the level of sensitivity from some of these people has somewhat been disappointing. I've learnt to eliminate toxic people out of my life, it's been easier for me to distance myself from these people rather than having to deal with their constant negativity.

I don't want to be pitied. It just gets under my skin. I may look fine, but the pain is permanent. Yes, I am and will always be, the chronically ill sick girl.

I wish I was active as you; I wish I didn't have to cancel plans,
but my health varies between the hour of the day... Believe me,
it's not something I can control.

Admittedly, I did isolate myself again from the people I love and respected the most. I created a lot of distance between us, and I am not proud of my actions and behaviour. *I was angry and hurt that I had relapsed so quickly. I was no longer in control...* I didn't feel good about myself and it seemed easier to avoid people, instead of calling them back, texting to meet up for coffee or lunch, dropping in for a casual visit, or go watch a movie together. I felt defeated

I feel so trapped by what is happening to me, I forget the impact
this is having on others. I am not happy how things turned out.

It hit me hard that I needed a holiday away from work, my routine and the stressors of Scleroderma, I took two weeks off work and flew to Singapore. The weather was very warm, and I spent most of my days sitting by the pool sipping on my cocktail. By night, we'd explore the city of Singapore and learn about the culture, making our way to street markets, Marina Bay Sands & Gardens By the Bay, then on to Universal Studios, followed by the Singapore Flyer, then making our way to Buddha Tooth Relic Temple and Museum and finishing up at Little India. There was so much to see, the city is big and spread so evenly; we wanted to experience as much as possible. With my converse shoes on, we walked on foot, travelling from one place to another. It took toll on my sore feet, causing stiffness and pain, later we'd jump on the MRT or grab a taxi to our next destination.

My life holds a purpose.

Scleroderma had become so visible. *It stole my beauty.* I wore makeup to cover up the red patches on my face. I have missing patches of hair in my eyebrows, my hair is thinning and I now have a beak shaped nose. To my disappointment, I have lost my lips to Scleroderma. I also have vertical lines above my lips and deep lines around my mouth. *It's disappointing how much scleroderma has changed the way I look.* I have become very self-conscious of my appearance and how I am perceived others. Especially those that know me so well.

I've been trying so hard to be strong for myself and others, but it's been tough fighting this incurable disease.

But today I remain wounded... I am breathing but my heart aches.

It seemed like everything about my face was suddenly changing for the worse. Once again, I have no control of these physical changes. I have always been high maintenance girl, so it was important for me to maintain my hair, makeup and nice clothes. But my face suddenly changed and there is no other fixed solution other than plastic surgery which I simply cannot afford, I am not rich. I am young, I love my face and I've always looked after my appearance, but I had no faith in cosmetic procedures to maintain this look.

There is a long line of attractive women in my family, we have very good genes and I could not accept I was losing my good looks to Scleroderma.

I constantly dealt with the challenges with my body and face. I waste so much time fixating on my scleroderma face, I felt trapped in my own cycle of negative thoughts, obsessing over my physical appearance of trying to fit into an image of how I am supposed to look. At one stage I shift my focus to others and wonder how they may perceive me. Do they think I am attractive? Do men find me desirable? Am I sexy? Am I good enough?

I hate that Scleroderma has stolen my beauty but I remind myself I am a strong woman and this will not break me and I have Allah to thank for that. This is the body and face that is given me that I am meant to grow old with and that I need to appreciate that everything about it is beautiful, *I am strong enough to live with it.*

One day I was driving home, I pulled over to the left and I cried helplessly. I just wanted to be free of Scleroderma and the pain I endured in my heart. Some nights I had cried myself to sleep, and then the following morning I'd wake up, apply my makeup and do my hair and get through my day with a smile, knowing that Allah is always with me.

It was simpler for me to accept myself unconditionally. I will never be free of scleroderma. I identify myself now as adequate in my current state. The self-criticism had to stop, I had to stop hurting myself. If my family and friends could accept me as I am, then why couldn't I accept myself and work with the belief I am good enough? I had to stop telling myself that I couldn't do this, *stop the negative talk, I cried today but tomorrow is a new day, giving up is not an option, I am worthy of lot more,* instead of constantly judging myself that was eating away at my confidence. I needed to accept that I had done the best I could to manage and deal with this disease and I will avoid repeating all this negative self-talk in the future. I had to make some improvements to the way I perceived myself.

There is more meant for me than this sadness that lurks in my heart. I had this need to validate myself by being perfect in the eyes of others and in my own shadow. What I learnt is that I needed to be kind and true to myself instead.

While I was watching my life unfold, I was still waiting for something great to happen, waiting for that greatness to occur. I've slowly learnt that Allah's plans did not align with any of my plans. No doubt this is the path Allah wants me to take, I have found acceptance in the direction I am walking somewhat the right path for me with no expectations.

I put together a coping mechanism that will help me deal with everyday challenges I encounter with the disease. This will be my breakthrough to help me transform into a better version of myself.

My Self-Acceptance Guide

- Write a journey about my experience with scleroderma

- Let go of what's hurting my heart and soul

- Take ownership of my life, confront my fears

- Find my strength and never lose sight of what I am capable of

- Believe in myself, I survived the worst and made this far

- Accept who I am

- Accept my flaws and imperfections

- Be patient, be kind

- Practise self-love — like and love myself. Respect and forgive myself

- Avoid self-criticism

- Reframe from thinking negative thoughts and replace them with positive thoughts

- Write positive inspirational messages, hang them on my mirror and bedroom wall and read them every day.

- Write self-assurance messages, to remind myself that what I am experiencing will pass

- Grieve the loss of unachieved dreams

- ○ Surround myself with good people and remove toxic people out of my life

- ○ I deserve to be HAPPY

- ○ SMILE

I will make do with my current state.... this is who I am supposed to be

My wellness care plan for dealing with Scleroderma

- ○ **Mental health**

  - Most important point is to get OUT OF BED before 10am

  - Change my mindset to help me feel better about myself: Rewire my thoughts

  - Replace negative thoughts with positive ones. There is no room for self-pity and hate

  - Maintain positive attitude, can do approach

  - Labels can hurt, so cruel name calling is not right. Don't be afraid to look at my reflection in the mirror, compliment myself

  - Focus on what good I can do and how it will make me feel

  - Embrace what I have achieve and how far I have come

  - Learn to love and respect myself

  - Don't compare myself to others

  - Learn to appreciate how beautiful I am in and out - perfection does not exist.

- Revaluate my life, set achievable goals and see them through

- Do things to help increase my confidence and self-esteem

○ Emotional Development

- Understand/recognise my worth and value

- Understand my feelings, emotions and how they may affect my thoughts and behaviour. Don't be afraid to express how I are truly feeling. Don't suppress my feelings.

- Alleviate my stress

- Set achievable goals but expect setbacks

- Keep a journal - describe how I am feeling and what steps I need to take to manage the stress, anxiety and endless pain, OR write a book about my battles with Scleroderma, write for myself and give myself time to grieve.

○ **Physical health – Wellbeing (Exercise and healthy eating)**
Physical health is vital for your well-being

- Rest and sleep – short naps to help rejuvenate the body, sleeping is essential for mind and body functionality

- Maintain a healthy diet - eat well balanced foods, avoid sugar and fatty processed meals – see Dietician if you must

- Eat more fruits and vegetables

- Mediate and breathing exercises for 20 minutes – clear your mind

- Regular exercises to improve your joints – strengthen muscles, flexibility and mobility

- Go to the gym - help to improve my mental health , well-being and boost my circulation

- Get regular massages

- Avoid smoking

o **Personal Hygiene**

- Shower daily

- Brush and floss my teeth

- Wear clean clothes

o **Spiritual guidance** *Seek comfort spiritually*

- Find my faith and Embrace it

- Pray religiously

- Establish peace

- Go to church, mosque, temple etc.

- Read the Bible or Quran

o **Social Interaction / Support Network**

- Explain the nature of the disease, how it is affecting my body. Explain to family and friends what I need from them. Be clear so they can understand and can manage their expectations

- Accept support — don't be afraid to speak up, express my feelings and emotions to family and close friends but also connect with support groups, share my experience, learn about other people's experiences

- Important to engage with others — work with the local

community, volunteer your time and raise awareness about the disease

- Interact more with family and friends (make an effort to attend social functions and gatherings, send a message, make a call)

- Speak to a therapist if I must

○ **Intellectual and occupation**

- Return to work with doctor's approval

- Going back to work will help to boost my confidence and self-esteem

- Important to work at a pace that suits my needs

- Give myself time for my body and mind to heal itself before I return to work

- Work at my comfort level and find balance

- Consider part time and gradually work my way up

- Some of us may not be able to return to work, never lose sight of what I can learn in your own time, open my mind to learn new things.

- Create my own blog: share my story

- Write a book, journal or poems, whatever helps to contribute to my wellness

- Be creative

Do things I actually enjoy:

○ Listen to my favourite music

- ○ Read

- ○ Watch funny shows and movies help to enlighten my mood

- ○ Go shopping

- ○ If I can, plan a trip

- ○ Go fishing

- ○ Attend a concert

- ○ Do some gardening

- ○ Play an instrument

- ○ Dance

- ○ Do a puzzle

- ○ Paint, cook

- ○ Explore nature and environment – its healing process

Although my life is not everything I envisioned it would be, I will not call it quits. Some days I won't be able to control how I feel, but I will not let this disease break me. I will continue to follow my care plan, lean on my family, friends and faith for guidance and support. I will continue to remain true to myself. I am me, but my story is messy, but it's what's got me here. I am a Scleroderma warrior. I will keep smiling while I am still breathing. I am forever hopeful.

PART 14: YEAR 2020

I LOST MYSELF last year; I was conflicted. Now I am stronger, beautiful and much wiser than ever, brave enough not to lose myself to scleroderma. I have flaws I am not perfect. I am not in competition with anyone. I accept the things I cannot change and am loving myself. This is my life and I am responsible for it. For me I am here, I am trying and that is enough for me. It took me a long time to love myself and I now feel I am in the process of becoming a better version of myself.

I am managing my symptoms relatively well, however the level of uncertainty remains. Will I have another 10 years to live? I will embrace the uncertainty, find beauty in the moments and joy in the story I am living. This is my journey, where nothing is certain and anything is possible. I will not surrender to the essence of uncertainty.

The power of wearing makeup

OK confession time... Part of my daily ritual when I wake up every morning is to apply my makeup and lots of it. I admit I look really pretty with makeup on. It increases my self-confidence, self-esteem and performance. It's the added boost I need to feel more physically attractive. It makes me feel good about myself and improves my image. Don't get me wrong, I appreciate my natural face but I will never the leave the house without makeup on. I feel drawn to it. When I apply makeup, my wounds are hidden. When I am not wearing makeup, I demonstrate the need for empathy; my pain is open to the public, my soul is exposed to all and I feel vulnerable in my current state. I know it's strange, but make up is my disguise and front face for scleroderma. I feel I can express myself freely, confront my fears and embrace who I am and where I want to be.

My beauty is average, there is nothing fancy about it.

The power of makeup also helps me to face the world. Not wearing it gives me anxiety. I use it for myself, not for others, and it enhances my appearance. Even when I am running late for work, I always apply my makeup in the car or the train. Either way, my makeup bag is always with me wherever I go. Makeup makes me feel different, it helps me to express myself and my identity. I must admit I look very different without makeup on and I accept I am a better looking person with makeup on. Honestly when I look in the mirror, I see a transformation; I am impressed with the power of makeup, and it's an improved new version of me. Wearing makeup is my choice, it's more of a self-fulfilling prophecy that I know I can be the better version of myself with makeup on, feeling confident in my own skin. Makeup may be a tool to enhance my features but it definitely contributes to my success and individuality.

When Scleroderma strikes - changes to my physical appearance:

Body

Prior to the transplant, I lost some weight. I was 58 kilos and I dropped down to 42 kilos. I was flat chested, and I lost my natural curves. I was all skin and bones. My body has changed, my curves are back so *YAY* for me, but my current weight is under 60 kilos. My hair has grown back thicker than usual, not that I am complaining, and the shape of my nose has changed, which is one of physical changes with Scleroderma.

Lips

HERE IS MY BIGGEST DILEMMA... I am still very self-conscious about my lips. I have always had reasonably full lips. I actually have a nice shape to my lips... So you can imagine how I devastated I was when I lost my lips to Scleroderma. I am desperate to have them back. I now have vertical lines above my lips, because my skin is still very tight around my mouth, and my mouth has shrunk, making it extremely hard for me to open my mouth wide. As such, I decided to experiment with lip fillers made up of hyaluronic acids such as Restylane and Juverderm.

After extensive research, I found myself sitting in the consultation room of a cosmetic clinic in Sydney. I sat down with the doctor to explain my medical condition and what I was hoping to achieve I explained to him it was very important for me to leave his clinic with a full volume of lips to enhance what was already there. Prior to the procedure, the doctor applied a numbing anaesthetic cream to my lips. Twenty minutes later he returned to the operating room to inject 0.6mls of Restylane in the upper lip and 0.4 mls in the lower lip, *it hurts like hell*. Within seconds, I was teary. The whole injecting process was awful. The doctor repeatedly apologised for making me cry. Getting jabbed in the mouth with a needle for the next twenty minutes was torture. Some will call this a very risky or desperate move. I would agree this was a desperate move, but I was desperate enough to believe it would actually work. The doctor was extremely gentle with the whole injecting process. Overall, it was the worst experience ever. My lips were swollen, sore, and I was bleeding excessively. Thirty minutes later, my eye makeup was all smudged and running down my face, but I was relieved the procedure is finally over. The doctor gently massages my lips to smoothen out the bumps and applies an ice-pack to help reduce the swelling. The results are instant. The doctor handed over a mirror, I looked into the mirror to see my reflection; I was amazed with the results, the filler had plumped my lips; they had taken shape and looked very natural. I couldn't believe these were my lips.

Two days later there was still some discomfort as I struggled to eat and drink. There were a few lumpy parts which were just bits of the fillers that were supposed to dissolve on their own. Instead, three weeks later the fillers in the top and bottom lip dissolved, leaving no trace of the fillers at all. My deflated lips were back again, and it was clearly a waste of money.

My desire to have full lips does not end here.

In July 2018, I consulted with a plastic surgeon from Bondi Junction who specialises in fat grafting. I had to explore all options, so I did some research on fat grafting to the lips. The procedure involves extracting small amounts of fat from one area of the body (abdomen, hip, stomach, thigh) after cleansing the fat, the fat is injected into the lips, a procedure known as autologous fat transfer. The fat will be used to break down the fibrosis around the mouth, weaken the muscles which will improve facial features such as mouth opening/widening of the lips. The procedure is costly and starts from $5,000 - $8,000 but is proven to be safe for my condition. There is one major drawback with this procedure. The extracted fat may only last up to six weeks or longer, it's a lot of money to lose for only six weeks. I consulted the second opinion of a plastic surgeon from Sydney Bondi Junction with over fifteen years of experience. As means to maintain his youth he had injected so much Botox into his face, he looked like a Ken doll. It was unnatural and his face was frozen, his whole face was virtually anti-wrinkle free and I found it difficult trying to read his emotions. He insisted on slicing my top lip to inject the fat in. When I heard the word slice, I was on my feet and ready to leave. The third encounter was with a plastic surgeon with over 22 years of experience from Sydney CBD Broadway. Very friendly guy with good bedside manner, all natural and free of Botox but he had plans of injecting 8-10 mls of fat into my top lips followed by 6-7 mls into bottom lip, that would most likely erupt my lips and move me into intensive care unit at the hospital.

And so my research continued....

I came across an alternative solution for lip enhancing called Permalips Implants. Permalips is a silicone-based product that is fitted into the lips. Permalips comes in different sizes and volumes, and are guaranteed to last for many years. Unlike fillers with lumps and hardening, Permalips gives a soft, natural look to the lips and is proven to be safe for Scleroderma patients. This type of treatment is not used in Australia but very common across Europe. Guess that won't be happening.

Fingers–hand impairment

Systemic Scleroderma can cause extreme deformity to the fingers. In late August 2018, I met with an occupational hand specialist to begin treatment on my claw-like fingers to regain motion and improve functionality. Hand therapy includes motion exercises and experimenting with handmade splints to wear (day/night) that would help to strengthen the muscles in my hands and fingers, stretch, enhance mobility and relieve the pain as much as possible. Four months later, I found these treatments to be ineffective and experienced no improvements to my hands and fingers whatsoever.

PART 15: LATE 2020/2021

Life is Gift

I want to live life and make the most of what I have… I don't know what today or tomorrow may bring, for now I am content. There is so many wonderful things around that I am thankful for. I will never settle. I will live in the moment and fill my life with joy, laughter and love. My experience with Scleroderma has brought me closer to my faith; my soul is no longer drifting. I no longer fear death—my struggle with scleroderma is just one part of my journey in life.

My life may not be perfect but I am OKAY with that.

To be a better version of myself

MY EXPERIENCE WITH Scleroderma has helped me to re-evaluate the way I perceive myself, I am finally able to accept my appearance. I look at myself in the mirror and see all the positive things about myself and I have finally stopped comparing myself to others. I will work with the belief I am good enough, and build on it, even if it takes some time. *I accept I am imperfect and vulnerable at times, but self-acceptance has made things a lot easy for me.* I got to a point where I stopped doubting myself. I began dismissing any negative thoughts and acknowledging my strengths and find comforting with my weakness. I realised I didn't need to be perfect or beautiful to be heard, respected and listened to, or to succeed and gain the things I wanted in life.

I accept I may need a few layers of makeup to look as a healthy individual. It's taken me a very long time to realise I am BEAUTIFUL even with all these differences. The issue with thin lips currently remains a hot topic. Reducing my insecurities, increasing my confidence and finding comfort with my image has been tough and quite challenging, it's been a process of ups and downs. As such, I have grown to be very fortunate with what I have and I know that it could have been much worse. I've seen what scleroderma can do to a person's face and it is not something pretty.

I came to realise that true beauty can only be found within.

In fact, I am *OKAY* that bad things have happened to me. There are new exciting things waiting for me that require my energy, attention and focus.

I see life differently now. I am slowly learning to find happiness and joy for the smallest things. The transplant has affected me in many ways, but I have been received the greatest gift of all, a second chance at life. I know my boundaries. I now understand my body, what works and what doesn't. Despite of what I am going through, I am hopeful to live a long life, to get married, have my own child or adopt a child and embrace all the happy days, special moments and events still waiting for me.

It's not easy for anyone to be in such a position, but as humans we must learn to adapt and grow from our life-changing experiences and stand strong. Scleroderma may have hijacked my life, but I can finally say I am no longer lost with the disease. By accepting what has happened to me, I have become more grounded, realistic, and practical.

I understand the suffering that comes with the disease and I admire my scleroderma brothers and sisters that have the strength and courage to get out of bed every morning and continue to move forward with their lives or anyone that is living with autoimmune diseases or chronic pain.

Being able to switch off and not dwell on the negativity of the disease is important… but embrace whatever comes your way, finding the goodness in the smallest thing, keeping a positive attitude, finding acceptance either today or tomorrow is a process and one step towards healing and inspiring to never give up and live life graciously. Learning to accept yourself begins with confronting your insecurities, accepting your inadequacies, stop comparing yourself to others and judging yourself, and finally demonstrating some self-compassion and self-affirmation to become the person you are supposed to be. Being comfortable with yourself is all that matters.

This is the path I must take, regardless of how it makes me feel. Accepting has helped me to let go of my past life plans and accepting the plans that are waiting for. I have acknowledged that the present situation is my chosen path. It took a long time for my heart to accept this when my mind knew this all along.

When I can let go of who I was and embrace the person I am meant to be, then something great will emerge.

My research with scleroderma continues

I am always still more learning more about the disease and finding better ways to treat / manage my symptoms. I came across an interesting article about an antibiotic protocol called Minocycline. The findings suggest Scleroderma is caused by infectious microbe (bacterial agent in the bloodstream).

According to a theory proposed by Doctor Thomas McPherson Brown from 1930s, Minocycline may be effective in eliminating this infectious microbe, killing the organism. Along with other antibiotics, Dr Brown theorised that these types of drug may help in the eliminate Rheumatoid Arthritis and treat rheumatoid diseases. These drugs may also have an anti-inflammatory effect. This is one man's theory, and many argued that Dr Brown held unorthodox views.

I made an appointment with my local family doctor hoping he would prescribe the aforementioned drug. I am happy to report that I have been using minocycline for the last three months and found positive improvements with my skin and fingers, and I am still currently using it. The ulcers have reduced which is surprisingly good.

My life still moves with a purpose

Year 2020

I've lived with Scleroderma for the last five years and every day I feel like my body is fighting a constant battle with itself. But I am a firm believer this is my fate. I've learnt to embrace the unexpected and trust this is Allah's plan. I will allow my life to unfold naturally and see where I end up.

Rediscovering my faith has helped me to restore my heart and soul. It has elicited feelings of hope, compassion, happiness and gratitude. Allah has helped me to face adversity head on, provided comfort in my struggles, helped me reflect on who I am as a person, lessen my fear of death and helped me make better choices. Thanks to Allah, I've found acceptance in my own skin, been inspired me to live courageously, and to maintain a positive outlook on life experiences even if I don't anticipate them. Allah has given me the resilience to adapt and adjust when faced with change.

My faith comforts me in my daily struggles, despite my exhaustion.

I feel my faith has helped me to become a better version of myself, and I am more equipped to handle everyday challenges. I understand bad things may happen to me, some things may not be in my control, but there is more to life than just giving up. Religion will always be an important part of my life.

To this day, I find myself praying with all my heart, being thankful for seeing the light of day and family is plenty and enough.

My faith helps me to become more flexible and relaxed into life.

I feel this disease has also changed my family. We all look at life differently now, and I've learnt to appreciate and value each moment I spend with them. I hold a big gratitude to my family. They witnessed my anguished pain and suffering with scleroderma and realised there is little they can do to make it go away. But their ongoing support and unconditional love continues to inspire me to not give up and keep pushing forward. I am forever grateful to them all. If I didn't have the love and support of my family, I wouldn't be the person I am today.

To this day, I am not using Cellcept to slow down the progression of the disease. My lung functionality continues to remain stable and I am still hopeful that I will be able to commence with IVF when the time comes. I am using Oregano Oil daily to ease the chronic cough, which has not been as helpful as I initially hoped.

I am always trying to find ways to improve my appearance. With that been said, I did some research and found a cosmetic surgeon with over 45 years of experience to seek his medical opinion for fat grafting to help restore my lips. My first consultation went well, we discussed my medical health condition, my expectations and answered any questions I may have. He proposed injecting 3-4 mls in the top and bottom lip to slow build up the volume at an afford-able price and to repeat the following steps in a few months' time at no additional cost, until I achieved the desired results. On the day of the procedure, I was sitting in the surgeon's consultation room looking at my lips for one last time and thinking to myself ... *this is really happening...* I was excitedly nervous but extremely worried at the same time about the amount of grafted fat I requested to be injected into my lips. *Would it be too obvious? Would they look kind of fake and ducky?*

Harvesting the fat from my thigh was probably the worst part of fat grafting. I could feel the occasional jab as he extracted the fat. I bruised at the injecting sites around my mouth and thigh. Immedi-ately after the operation, my mouth and chin were incredibly swollen and were so numb.

Two weeks later, my puffiness around my mouth had slightly dropped. By the third week the swelling had eased and my lips looked extremely natural. I was impressed with the shape and volume. The lines around my mouth were no longer there. It certainly made a big difference to my face. Almost six weeks later, the fat had dissolved and my lips had returned to their deflated state, which was a known possibility. On my third attempt I agreed to have 1 ml of fat injected into my lips. To my disappointment it dissolved two weeks later.

As of April 2020, the coronavirus (COVID-19) struck globally. The outbreak of the COVID-19 pandemic changed our lives and continues to affect our everyday living and activities, and with more restrictions regularly being put into place. For four months I had been working from home, as the virus continued to spread. Millions of people worldwide were getting tested for COVID-19, and I had suddenly become one of them. By late July, I came down with the flu; runny nose, headache, sore throat and a chest infection. I drove to the nearest COVID clinic. I was approached by a woman wearing COVID protective gear suit and mask. She put an unpleasant swab up my nose which made my eyes and nose all watery and then a swab in the mouth which tasted a lot like garlic. They detected no trace of COVID, and my results came back negative and I was relieved. One less thing I didn't have to deal with but it was always an ongoing concern. I am taking extra precautions to avoid comprising my immunity.

Year 2021

My sister has kindly offered to donate her eggs so I can start a family of my own. I have been so overwhelmed with her generosity, but in the last few months I have had discussions with an IVF specialist from Royal Hospital Research Centre for women in Randwick and after a series of tests they detected two small follicles in my ovaries.

However, my decision to proceed with IVF currently remains on hold. It's not often you see an unmarried Muslim Lebanese girl adopt or conceive a child without a partner. That having been said, I have realised the best thing to do is to get married then commence with IVF process.

Could there be hope for me after all?

In the event of settling down and getting married, I leave this note here for my unborn child/adopted Inshallah.

To my unborn or adopted child,

I am sorry it's taken me this long to get my life together.

I'm breathing air but I'm choking on tears

Silence in my heart, I am raging with emotions

There is so much distance between us and a life time of uncertainty

I will remain sincere to you, your presence will unfold this silence and void in my heart, that weeps in your absence. It will bring tear of joy to my eyes and comfort to my fragile heart as I will hold you in my arms, loving you adoringly, shower you with kisses, tell you stories and sing you songs.

To my unborn or adopted child, patience eludes me but Allah will help me find my way and grace me with your presence. I will finally be content.

My little one, my sleeping child... is your name Ella-Nour or Noah?

I may not be able to carry you for the full term or carry you at all, but we will still have a connection.

I want to hear you cry... I want to see you smile... I want touch your soft skin... I pray we will meet someday

I want you to know you'll be the best thing that has ever happened to me.

Until then, I love you my precious child and I can't wait to meet you little one...

A year on and my chronic cough has not improved and it's only getting worse. I've been sleeping upright for a year now and avoiding large meals after 6pm. I am woken by a sudden cough that lingers for a good ten to fifteen minutes. It was in the early hours of the morning, when it was dark and quiet... not even the occasional creak of the house, or the sound of an animal or a car with a noisy motor exhaust driving up my street. It's hard to believe how silent it was. I leant over to switch on my bedside lamp, eagerly trying to find my inhaler as my coughing echoed through the hallway awakening my mother, who burst her way into my room to see me barfing up contents of food which hadn't digested well in my stomach. I was standing in my own puke, strings of hair dangling over my face. My nose started running and tears filled my eyes. I look over to mum. She told me it's going to be okay, that she will clean up the vomit. She urged me to go have a shower.

My recent visit with my lung specialist led to an endoscopy to examine my oesophagus, digestive system and a biopsy to collect tissue samples... A few weeks later, I was admitted as an outpatient into St Vincent's Hospital for the endoscopy procedure. My heart pounded as I entered through the sliding doors of the hospital, I distinctly noticed the smell. This was once my home. A wave of disappointment washed over me and I was faced with another flashback moment.

As we (mum and I) headed to the lift lobby, I pressed the arrow facing up and two to three minutes later we entered the elevator heading to level five. On arrival we headed toward the reception desk to inform the woman at the front desk of my arrival. My procedure was scheduled for 8:30am and I had been fasting for the last twelve hours and my stomach was making all kinds of noises. We've been sitting in the waiting room for the last hour, waiting for one of the nurses to come out and call my name... Five minutes later, my name was called out and a nurse apologised for the delay and handed over a plastic bag for my clothes and a hospital gown. Mum leant in to give me a big hug and a kiss goodbye as she was ushered away to the waiting area.

I walked over to one of the change rooms and began to undress. I stood there naked, looking at myself in my mirror. *A face of disappointment stared back at me,* holding a pair of disposable undies in one hand, reliving moments again. I had just changed into my hospital gown and panties, when I felt the cold air, an icy feeling comes over me. My fingers turned blue and I am shivering as I followed the nurse to the hospital bed. I climbed in and side rails go up. As I laid there with my eyes closed, I relived the moments six years ago… My thoughts were interrupted by a male nurse and some guy who will move my bed into the operating room. I am feeling anxious about the procedure; I am so nervous. My palms are all sweaty as my bed is wheeled through the hallways of the corridors to the operating room. I close my eyes and recite an Islamic pray to help calm my nerves, for Allah to protect me and return me home to my loved ones. As I open my eyes, nurses in blue and green uniforms move through the hallways. Some smile in my direction and I smile back.

I finally arrive at the theatre room where it looks all too familiar to me. I feel I have been here before in one of the rooms where a catheter was once inserted into my neck as a central line. I am greeted by friendly anaesthetist; she struggles to find a good vein in my left arm but soon manages to find a small vein in my left hand. Before she inserts the IV cannula, topical anaesthetic is applied to the skin. *I can't feel a thing.*

A mouth guard with a central hole is inserted into my mouth and was wrapped around my head to hold it in place. Seconds later, a Gastroenterologist slowly injects Propofol anaesthetic into the cannula to decrease my level of consciousness, but in that moment, which felt like hours to me I screamed in agony. Tears rolled down my cheeks as I cried out helplessly as he continued injecting propofol in the cannula. It felt like my left hand was been sawn off by chainsaw… then, I passed out and dreamt that I was back home sitting on the couch with one of my brothers and having a good laugh… as the anaesthetic wore off I overheard someone say *she has... poor thing...* and that is all I could remember.

When I finally woke up, the registrar Gastroenterologist walked over to the hospital bed to inform me that I had a mild case of Gastroparesis. They suggested doing a stomach emptying study. Six weeks later I was sitting in the clinic of St Vincent's Clinic with my mother for my follow-up appointment with the Gastroenterologist who performed the endoscopy, only to learn I had a bacterial infection commonly known as Helicobacter Pylori (which is treated and cured with antibiotics) a spiral bacterium which is found in the stomach causing irritation and inflammation of the stomach lining (not associated with Scleroderma). Something I might have eaten could have potentially caused this. That took my back to my holiday to Lebanon late 2008 when I was invited out for dinner and I ordered a vegetarian pizza. For the next few days I had a bad case of gastro and food poisoning and to return home six weeks later weighing only 49 kilos. Then five years later to be diagnosed with Scleroderma... Could it all be linked? Could this potentially be one of the underlining causes of Scleroderma? The endoscopy identified dilated oesophagus and scarring at the end of the food pipe, and an excessive amount of gastric fluid which is widely common in Scleroderma patients.

My recent follow up with my haematologist has suggested a procedure where a ring of tissue is placed end of the oesophagus to make it narrow, where food could easily pass through to the stomach and not make its way up through the oesophagus (triggering coughing and vomiting attacks) into my lungs causing permanent damage.

Nevertheless, I am managing Scleroderma relatively well. I am trying to live a healthy life: my routine consists of drinking daily smoothies made up of all greens (kale, spinach, cabbage, watercress mixed with berries and banana) and exercise twenty minutes a day on the cross trainer.

In my state of discomfort, I still manage to smile with confidence and laugh with others. I am no longer afraid of the disease or the uncertainty that comes with it. *My body no longer feels foreign to me.* I know my limitations. I've learnt to cope with these limitations and take one day at a time. I will not retire with the attitude that scleroderma owns my body and defines who I am.

Scleroderma may have hijacked my life, stolen my identity but it will *NOT* take away my chances of get married, having or adopting a baby, isolate me from the people I love, restrict me from doing the things I enjoy. It may be a big part of my life, but I will not allow this disease to consume our everyday living.

It is my job to stay alive.

The simple truth is, I don't really know where my path will take me. I have no timeline or roadmap of where I am going or where I will be in five or ten years from now, but I will live life to the fullest of what's left of it, and take proactive steps to ensure I live it well.

Every day on earth is a blessing and I want to make each day count. I will continue to maintain a healthy diet and exercise at my own pace and lean on my support system of family and friends, connect with people that make me feel good, plan ahead, set achievable goals, be hopeful that it will all come together.

I am just thankful I get to wake up every day.

If could be someone else for the day (free of Scleroderma), I'd still choose me. It's taken me a long time to love myself again... Somewhere along the way, I found beauty and comfort in my own skin and mastered self-confidence. It's taken a very long time for me to fall in love with myself and become my favourite person.

We can all manage with an uncertain future. My mission is to the support people living with Scleroderma as they embark on their journey with the disease and to help raise awareness.

Let's not focus on the severity of disease or ponder the uncertainty. So please make an effort to "GET OUT OF BED", live the sort of life you want to live, rediscover yourself and trust that everything will come together.

Believe me, nothing is impossible. Focus on the bigger picture and what really matters here. Set your mind and heart to it and never lose hope of what good may come to you. When you stop resisting and find acceptance, you will embrace all life experiences good or bad, it is then you will find true happiness within.

I did, because I simply didn't give up.

I hope my story will help you all to understand that maintaining a positive outlook in life will help you move forward with the disease. Don't be afraid to seek help from a professional, lean on your family and friends for support or join a support group. We are all in this together, we all have own our battles to fight and we don't need to go through it alone, help is available. One way or another, we are all connected. The struggle is real.

One day I woke up a different person. My faith gives me the courage, strength and determination to keep moving forward.

It is very important for me to not lose hope. I encourage you all to do the same. If you stumble and fall, get back up again, just take a deep breath and try again. Learning to live with Scleroderma becomes a lot easier and more manageable if you start believing in yourself that you can do this.

It takes a brave person to rebuild their life after being diagnosis with scleroderma.

The next step of this journey involves embracing my new path that Allah has intended for me. For now, this is the path that I will take to grow and evolve into a better version of MYSELF.

Before Scleroderma – Year 2013

Last Day at St Vincent's Hospital – With one of my brothers

Year 2021

Mum, dad and I – 2021

Rheumatologist: Dr Helen Englert and Ross Penglase

Haematologist: Dr John Moore

Plastic surgeon Dr Longin Zurek

Clawed Hands

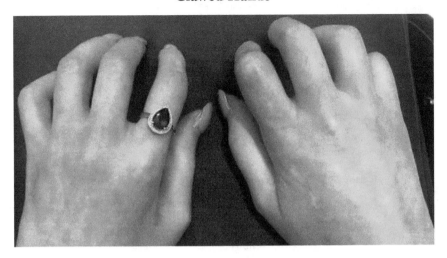

Year 2020 - Circular Quay Sydney

Shawline Publishing Group Pty Ltd

www.shawlinepublishing.com.au

SHAWLINE
PUBLISHING
GROUP

CPSIA information can be obtained
at www.ICGtesting.com
Printed in the USA
LVHW081334030721
691839LV00008B/640